Dedicated
to
Phyllis Playter

For why should others' false adulterate eyes
Give salutation to my sportive blood?
Or on my frailties why are frailer spies,
Which in their wills count bad what I think good?
No, I am that I am, and they that level
At my abuses reckon up their own :
I may be straight, though they themselves be bevel.

WILLIAM SHAKESPEARE

INTRODUCTION

The writing of Mr. Llewelyn Powys may be said to embody what has been since the time of William Langland characteristic of the best English prose. It is sturdy, innocent, philosophic, and impassioned, and it has beside running through it from beginning to end, like a silver thread on a royal cloak, something aerial and unexpected. It is especially English, as Matthew Arnold might have pointed out, in that the luxuriance of the imagery sometimes overbalances the main thought of the sentence, just as fruit too heavy on the branch may bear it down and mar the shapeliness of the tree. And yet it would be difficult to find in English literature any book with which this one of Mr. Powys' could be compared. It is a love story but not a novel, an autobiography which leaves us in doubt as to whether it is a true account of the author's life or not, and it is charged from beginning to end with a poetic fervour which lifts it immediately above what is contemporaneous and commonplace. True art is always aloof to praise or censure, it speaks from an inner flame into an outer silence ; and it is rich according to whether the artist's vision is rich, deep according to whether he has dwelt long enough, fearlessly enough, and patiently enough upon his own joys and sorrows to extract from each one its last reluctant truth, and whether he is able to present this unique personal vision in a form lucid enough and eloquent enough for others to share. Mr. Powys, where he has written of eternal things—of death, of the creation of animal and vegetable life, of the rapture of human consciousness—has written with the full force of his plenary imagination. The bright images that press upon his eager senses are transmuted into words that come swiftly and without effort to his pen and communicate to the reader the primal magic of his original impressions. There is in his writing nothing of the premeditated artist. There is not the conscious travail of thought, the artificiality of an over-strained attentiveness, the reluctance of the lagging blood to overtake an escaping insight. Mr. Powys expresses himself with his entire integrated nature, and of no one could it be better said that ' the style is the man.' He cannot write in a popular way for he can write only as he sees life, and he sees life as a countryman directly susceptible to every manifestation of the rude earth, as a sophisticated man of letters with an errant fancy apt at giving us those shocks of literary surprise that few but the initiated can justly value, and as a natural poet imbued with an earnest and vibrant knowledge of the ' warrantable' values of life.

It is only in those portions of his book in which Mr. Powys treats of his great love that we are at all conscious of the limitations that he shares with his compatriots. Here we feel that he has not always been sedulous to pursue the difficult truth, cold, unemotional, unimplicated, to its last retreat. In the unreliable morass of advance, flight, and duplicity called sexual attraction, it soon becomes clear that he has been content to pipe, like a shepherd boy upon a downland lawn, a love rhapsody passionate and poignant enough, but one which we suspect is not a wholly satisfying presentation of those rendings of the human heart that instruct our proud intellects, or send us prematurely to our graves. It is not the authenticity of his feelings that we doubt, there are cries that spring directly from his pages to us, but it is the implications of his own experience, and of the experience of the romantic girl of his choice, that we fancy have not been plumbed to their full depth ; and what countryside, let alone one that lies within the chalky ramparts of the decorous sea-girt island of his birth, has ever harboured, particularly in the era of which he writes, and in such provincial circles, so scholarly and emancipated a young lady of eighteen ?

And yet this novel that is not a novel can hardly be judged by the ordinary standards of fiction writing. Its stately dialogue, so grave, ceremonious, and ingenuous, resembles the conversations that might have taken place between Nicolette and Aucassin if they had left off their delicate dalliance to enter into sober moods of conference ; its background of flowery fields, mossy lanes, and silent ' Dancing Dells ' are like the landscapes in Hero and Leander, in Venus and Adonis, in Endymion ; even the River Yeo, of which Mr. Powys is so fond, becomes a kind of river of Shallot flowing through an ideal champaigne in some Chanson de Geste, until suddenly a real fish leaps crescent-backed out from a real splashing river. Indeed this alternation of a reality as actual and life-giving as a pan of maple sugar, as vital as a hooked eel, as unexpected as the pricked ears of a fox above a bed of ferns, with a dream-like unreality, as if we were looking at the reverse side of a child's coloured transfers, is characteristic of this singular book. It is old-fashioned and at the same time extremely modern, startlingly realistic and at the same time as elusive as the sus-pended glimpses travellers sometimes catch of twilight summer gardens through dark narrow porticos with the voices of playing children dying away upon the still air.

Is it too much to prophesy that this volume of my husband's with its timeless ballad-like quality, its innocent classic truths, its passionate spiritual serenity, and its rich exuberant store of natural poetry will be read and enjoyed by men and women long after his bones have come to dust, will be honoured, indeed, by all those people whose interest in literature is firmly grounded upon an ardent and philosophic love of life?

ALYSE GREGORY

LOVE AND DEATH

I

The state of man does change and vary,
Now sound, now sick, now blythe, now sary,
Now dansand mirry, now like to die :—
Timor Mortis conturbat me.

WILLIAM DUNBAR

THE SUN STOOD HIGH UP ABOVE ST. ALBAN'S HEAD.
It was the first of May and I had gone into the
stubble-field above my cottage to look at the
sea. As I walked across this field, stiff yet with the short
winter-weathered corn stalks of the last summer's harvest, I became conscious of an impulse to pray. Looking
about to assure myself that the downs were deserted, I
lay flat upon my belly with my arms stretched out before
me. With my eyelids close shut, I now gave myself up
to worship. To the worship of whom, of what? He
that weighs the wind must have a steady hand. I did not
believe in God. To imagine that the universe is subject
to any kind of surveillance has for many years seemed
to me a gross delusion. Unless rendered stupid by a
sprinkling of holy water a single hour of anybody's
experience of life should be enough to do away with
such a notion. An old ape hath a cunning eye. Closely

to observe the common happenings on a single acre of land raises innumerable objections to so easy a hypothesis.

Never, I hope, shall I teach my haggard and unreclaimed reason to stoop unto the lure of faith. For honourable worship, be it understood, the existence of God is in no way necessary. In such an exercise it is sufficient if the spirit of a man hold itself in suspension, hold itself poised under an awareness so passionate that the human conceptions of cosmogony become of little moment. When my bones ache in thankfulness for my creation and preservation, when the very hair upon my scalp tingles with life, I have found that I can get immediate release by falling upon the earth in some solitary place. On such occasions I acquire refreshment for my spirit by merely snatching at a fugitive consciousness of personal existence on the earth, of personal existence on this giddy-green, welladay planet. I feel the wind brush past my ears, I listen to the larks above my body, above my pliant notched spine and curved ribs ; I feel the pressure of the strong sustaining fallow land against my knees and against my forehead, and I know myself to be alive, happily alive upon the solid resistant tilth. On such occasions I can smell the smell of the earth as unmistakably as if I were lying with my nose clapped down upon the broad back of some wild boar, its bristly shoulders rank with its own health and the warmth of

the forest's steaming sunshine. While thus transported
by my confidence in sweating reality I keep casting my
mind into the outer spaces and then retrieving it. It is
not, however, easy to sustain for any length of time such
daring tercel flights, and on this morning I found that I
was very soon irrelevantly considering the rapidly chang-
ing shapes of light that kept appearing and transforming
and merging and vanishing upon the sensitive nerve-
screens of my fast-closed eyelids. What were the most
constant shapes of these fluctuating phantasmagoria of the
blinded retina? Always they were the shape of a bone
with its clumped articulating hinges clearly limned at each
of its ends. I would have preferred any other presentation
than this, putting me in mind as it did of a graveyard's
trash. My spirits would have responded eagerly, for instance, had it been a simple circle. This shape would have
been a shape of triumph—this shape, subtle as an amphis-
bæna, that had so fascinated the awakening discriminations
of primitive man with its free-flowing rhythm without
corners or end. The stone temples of primitive man were
constructed after its fashion, and later it became his fond
habit to endeavour to keep the troth of his lissom lady
by slipping a circle of gold upon her finger of frail dust,
with a 'Hey! Trolly, lolly, and God save you, Lady
Em!'

Never once, however, did this symbol of eternity come

before my shut eyes. It was when I was trembling with a simple happiness at the fact that my heart was still beating like the heart of any beast, like the heart of a lion, a trout, a mole, or cutty-wren, that I coughed and unmistakably tasted, deriving from somewhere at the back of my right lung, a sinister corruption. I had been for so long suffering from a whoreson consumption, and the history of my case had been so varied—with improvement following retrogression, and retrogression improvement—over a period of more than a quarter of a century, that I had been accustomed to experiencing moods of both depression and elation. This particular taste, however, as though black mud had been stirred up at the bottom of the no-bottom pond in the Trent woods, filled me with the grievous dismay that falls upon a man who, with his gust for living still unsatisfied, knows suddenly for certain that death is approaching. It is the recoil of the eyes against blindness, of the ears against deafness, of the sense of touch against insensibility. It is the impulsive drawing back of a mortal, cry havok ! havok ! havok! before the eternal nothingness of the grave.

2

ALL THROUGH THOSE WEEKS, THOUGH I HAD BEEN
suspicious of my health, I had never once taken steps
to discover the amount of my fever. I had been
reluctant, I think, to resume that punctilious vigilance
which of necessity had been my business for so many
years. I now ascertained for a surety that it was far
higher than it should be.

At once I realized that I must have allowed the sickness to get a new power and that the only thing to do
was again to concentrate my whole attention upon
my cure. 'Let the sick chick live though it hath the
pip.' I went to bed in my open-air revolving shelter
which stood at the end of the cottage garden overlooking
one of the great valleys of the Dorset downs, a valley
secluded, and even in sunny weather disturbed by little
else than the silent transitory shadows of ravens, seagulls,
and of the little flickering birds of the gorse-bushes, so
merry in song. Except for coming into the house to

5

wash, I did not get up again for five weeks. The fever responded immediately to the complete rest. As soon as it showed signs of improvement, I experienced the long hours of content that descend upon me always when I know myself to be conquering some fresh attack of my sickness, and am convinced that, once more, I am reprieved, and am escaping from my enemy to enjoy again, with a free heart, the evening sunshine on grass, on stone, on window, and on wall. I had been careless to allow this fresh activity to start, but undoubtedly, I thought, in all these years my constitution must have developed an obstinate resistance to the infection, and in future, now that I had had the warning, I resolved to be much more wary. 'There is a remedy for all things but death, which will be sure to lay us flat one time or other . . . as soon goes the lamb to the spit as the old wether.' I was in bed till the end of June. Before I was better the nasturtiums were in flower.

When at last I got up I altered my manner of living. I had heard of the benefits of sun-bathing, and every morning I would spend an hour and a half walking naked over the deserted downs—a tiny mite upon an enormous landscape. The sun continued to shine every day. It was a remarkably fine summer. I had always been happy and had always recognized that this should be the one aim to the attainment of which all individual spirits should direct their wills. The condition of happiness should be striven for with an unyielding resolution. To be malcontent and frustrated in life constitutes a sorrowful personal failure. Next the end of sorrow, anon entereth joy. We were not born to be miserable, not born to waste the gift of breath in murmuring at every jar like the Jews in the wilderness. He is wise enough that can keep himself warm. Always happiness must be won by hook or by crook.

It was as though the sun during my convalescence had turned my wits. I had always thought of myself as a child of the sun, and I certainly might have been said to have had Jack-a-dandy in my eyes that summer. Cardinal Newman somewhere declares that it is not natural for the human heart to love God ! If this be true, it is a good truth and a doughty one. But even so, there is room for worship when worship we must. If behind life's manifold shadows of terror and beauty there exists nothing, then it is to this nothing that, crooking the knee, I touch my forehead to the ground. Every morning I would kneel at the window like a Dorset Daniel plotting balls of pitch for dragons. In a few moments I would be able to detach myself from the day-by-day actuality and to see the garden with the frenzied eye of a poet—the swallows brabbling on the top railing, the tiny-

7

winged, early morning flies. 'I asked the prophet Isaiah how he dared so roundly to assert that God spoke to him, and Isaiah answered, " I saw no God nor heard any in a finite organical perception, but my senses discovered the infinite in every thing." ' In a flash, the familiar cottage enclosure would become undulled by use and wont, and I would be able to envisage the small birds as winged vertebrates incredibly created with filament-ridged pennants to skim through the air, adroit to balance at a moment's notice on cherry-tree, on fence, or quince-tree branch, as though at liberty in paradise ; and the smell of sweet-peas would come up to the open window, and the smell of the innumerable green leaves of the flowers, and the smell of wet-spreading roots pressing into the earth. I would then hear the hum of existence, and my spirit would fly free in an ecstasy, in a kind of dancing fealty to the eternity in time that I was experiencing. I would look down upon the huge red blossoms of the Persian poppies, some of them only half open, with dew-sparkling hairy green calyxes lying on tight-folded petals, like eggshell fragments waiting to fall from the back of some motionless chick, a chick featly feathered in royal scarlet, a wonder for men to see !

On such occasions I would feel compelled to worship with my mind and with my quick flesh the spectacle of precarious life.

8

The eternal law, the deep life-stream,
Why should I worship these?
Better the briefest human dream
Among the fading trees!

Better the frailest human touch
When the harebells cover the hill,
Or the broken memory of such
When the heart has had its will!

This impulse would come upon me sometimes when I was talking with people in my upstairs parlour with words of little meaning. Suddenly I would be compelled to go out to some unseen place, a Judas-eared elder patch perhaps, or a hawthorn-tree bowed by the sea winds, and to abandon myself to these peculiar devotions of my own. A wise and truly religious man ought never to pry into the secrets of heaven. Though my mind had long turned obstinate after the nature of a thistle-eating ass, yet my bones, my marrow-bones, remembered perhaps the old ways of my fathers and continued to practise the traditional attitude, as I have seen a wasp make a to do upon a fruit-plate with head cut off. The older the Welshman, the more madman. This compulsion towards experiencing heightened consciousness when it came upon me I was forced to obey. Its commands would be suddenly strong as the urge of the physical necessities of my body, and as insistently troubling to my spirit as the stir in the heart of a woodcock during the days before migration. Real religion is no doting delusion. It is to pray to a purpose as priests praise God in the morning. It has nothing to do with morality and little enough to do with man's theological haverings. Where, then, is it to be found ? The mould of the earth gleams with the radiance of it as does also the dust in the moon shining above the sagebrush bush that shelters the prairie-dog's tunnelled home in the deserts of far Arizona. It is in the flash of the goatsucker's eye, in the luminosity of the glow-worm's tail, and in the phosphorescence of the equatorial wave, with its shoulder for an instant smoothly poised under the light of Canopus. It is the cosmic ray whose inspired shiver penetrates to the heart of the oak and of the rock. 'For the stone shall cry out of the wall and the beam out of the timber shall answer it.' It is the living cry of each conscious mind, calling ducdame ! ducdame ! ducdame ! to the stars as like a widgeon it flies through the night upon the wings of a wild enfranchisement.

How exultantly I honoured the sun that hot summer, god of triumphant life, rising in his giant's strength morning after morning ; shining down upon the hayfields red with sorrel, upon the ripening corn golden against the blue of the channel, upon banks of sweating seaweed lying along the shingle, where, with dexterous scratching claws and nebs of faultless application, sea-salt wet, the rooks and daws congregated to search for the worms and maggots of their appetites, that, conditioned to a lowly consciousness, rove and lurk amid the steaming wrack.

3

Hey, nonny no !
Men are fools that wish to die !
Is't not fine to dance and sing
When the bells of death do ring ?

ANONYMOUS

I HAD NEVER KNOWN A SUMMER IN ENGLAND AS HOT AS
this summer, unless, possibly, it was my summer with
Dittany Stone. Walking about naked my body became
berry-brown. A pair of screech owls nested in the barn.
This was of great interest to me. One of the little birds
fell on to the floor. Apparently its mother, thinking all
her young to be beauties, still kept it supplied with food.
I was never tired of going to see it, this ball of white pontifical fluff ! I would hold it in my hands. It would not
be frightened but would remain perfectly still, patient and
haughty. It resembled a bird Bishop dressed in an alb
of marabou feathers, and well could I imagine it being
summoned to administer last unction to an ailing corn-bin
fairy. The outlandish countenance of this fledgeling of
the dark night bewitched my attention. Its unexpected
appearance never failed to make me feel as if there were

12

another land close by, very close ; to be reached by the gravest mortal with a crooked hop 'in the third part of a minute.' With Long Will I cudgelled my brains to know where the magpie learnt to lay the sticks that make her nest, hiding and covering it that no fool should find her eggs, and how the water-fowl was taught to dive in the marshes. 'Dear God, where gat these wild things wit ?' How could such an amazing creature as the nestling owl be regarded usually ? And yet its extraordinary presence was taken for granted—a young moon-screecher on the floor of a barn, of an ordinary barn, that smelt of damp straw and dust-motes !

I grew better every day now and I could walk down to the village. One morning, as I was about to turn into the lane below Church Farm, I caught sight of the shepherd at the door of his cottage. This old man had been shepherd for as long as I could remember. I had passed him in all weathers out on the downs. He was a bachelor. His greatest friend had been an old bee-wife who lived in a cottage behind The Sailor's Return. This woman, whom we all so liked, and who each spring would laugh like a woodpecker to see her bees swarm, had fallen sick in the winter. She grew so thin that she could stretch out her skin six inches from her bones and let it back with a snap as though it had been elastic. Even in her sickness her eyes still remained as blue as periwinkles and she would still smack her thighs with merriment when I jested with her on country matters on Chaldon Green. Before she died of a malignant internal growth the news had gone about that the shepherd also had developed the same malady, for there had suddenly risen up on his jaw an inoperable cancer. In a village no dramatic event is ever lost ; the fact that this shepherd had followed the coffin of the beekeeper with a bandage about his chops, was not missed.

That bright summer morning when I caught sight of the old man I turned obstinately up the lane. I shrank from going to him, and yet I could not walk away at my ease. There seemed something unworthy about hurrying back to the blessed silence of the downs without a word to so familiar an acquaintance, so desperately trapped. I went back to the cottage door. The old man had a broom in his hand. He was evidently much pleased to see me. When I had first heard of his sickness I had given him some beer. After we had shaken hands he thanked me for the present. It was an effort for him, but he did it very earnestly as if he was determined to make me understand the genuine gratitude he felt ! He was a rough man who could make the beautiful daisy-covered hills—eloquent of the ' moods of God '—ring and ring again as he shouted curses at his curtal dog. Often and often I had heard him *swear at the wind* when at the time of the January lambing

a gale would come driving in from the cliffs so strong
that he would hardly be able to reach the fold of straw-
matted hurdles, would indeed be forced to stand stock-still
with a lamb dangling from each hand and the ewe close
by with her after-birth swinging at every gust.

I was touched now to see tears in his eyes. I asked him
if he suffered much pain. He answered, ' The nights be
the worst.' We stood talking in the passage-way of his
cottage which smelt of the dust he had disturbed with
his besom. Suddenly he made the very suggestion that
I most dreaded. ' Wouldn't 'ee like to look at 'en ? '
He spoke with animation, as if he had had a pink-
eyed ferret to show me. My hesitation was evidently
apparent, for as he removed the bandage, pulling it over
his round grey head with the same motion that a child
might use who has been playing blindman's buff, he tried
to reassure me by saying, ' 'Twon't turn your stomach,
never fear.' The cancer was an ugly object to look at.
The decaying flesh had suppurated into a kind of circle
suggestive of a volcano with a sinister crater in its centre.
At the bottom of this abyss of putrid decaying matter the
white of the jaw-bone was visible. I was surprised at the
calmness with which I could contemplate so revolting a
wound.

And yet when I left the shepherd and began to walk up
the lane between the hedges of wild plum, which in the

15

blaze of the August noon cast so cool a shadow, I experienced a feeling akin to shame. To be alive and not immediately menaced seemed so God-like a condition. As I passed pensive on my way, I understood very clearly the propulsion that drives heroical-minded women and men to extremes of self-sacrifice.

> *The wild owl over the mad-house knows*
> *In what padded place*
> *The loveliest form that ever breathed*
> *Lies on her face.*

A disastrous flood keeps surging down upon the happy homesteads of the world and surely every honourable man and woman must put before everything the damming back of this drowning torrent of sickness and misery. Sanctity is grounded upon passion and by means of the sublimation of love mortals will challenge the powers of hell. Certain I am that Saint Francis, and the wise Gatama, would have washed the shepherd's corrupting wound ; while Jesus would have torn up his seamless shirt to make linen pads to dress it, for the bandage the old man had removed from his head had not been as white as the may blossom. ' Never lighter was a leaf upon a linden tree, than thy love was when it took flesh and blood of man, fluttering, piercing as a needle-point.'

By the time I had reached the top of Chalky Knap I

had, however, recovered better sense. ' For who knoweth what is good for man in his life, all the days of his vain life which he spendeth as a shadow ? ' I understood in a flash, being filled with furious insolence, that the true employment of a free man, the profound purpose of his life should be to increase the sum of *his own happiness* in all hours, and in all places, each yellow-hosed bachelor after his fashion eagerly progging for his own joy. Self-love is the measure of our love to our neighbours. If it is possible for such a one to relieve suffering here and there, as, with an imaginative, far-seeing, experienced eye, he advances on his triumphant way, so much to the good, but on no account must he allow his own proud life-avowals to be betrayed. The war between cruelty, stupidity, and oppression, and generosity, intelligence, and freedom is as never ending as that waged between the pygmies and the cranes, and the issue as uncertain. Wherever a man dwell he shall be sure to have a thorn-bush near his door. Good and evil are as integral a part of life as are light and darkness. Trusty Robins and Little Johns and Scarlets, we must be using our quarter-staffs to a purpose when occasion offers, and then, back again to the good greenwood where are freedom, and flowers, and the wild red deer. A human being has but a few years of life and then once more oblivion. The abstinences solicited by the unique madness of the cross cannot be sanctioned by the wise. They do a deep damage to man's natural gift for spontaneous happiness. The black threads of suffering and death are inextricably woven into life's arras, and they can only be accepted with sense and sanity if outnumbered by the gilded threads of joy. Every man for himself and God for us all.

Nothing could ever make me forget that Thursday. It was the third of August. There were no clouds in the heavens. In the afternoon I took off my shirt and jacket, and naked to the waist, spent the hours gardening, weeding the flower-bed this side of the cat's kennel I had made. Dry as it was, I could smell the soil as I turned it up and with tugging fingers pulled at the long bindweed roots. After we had had supper on the terrace and had spent half an hour watering flowers in the garden, I felt restless. The night air was so warm that I still wore no shirt. Both the owls were out. I had seen them go wavering over the slates of the great barn. ' They say the owle was a Baker's daughter. Lord, we know what we are, but know not what we may be. God be at your Table.' Suddenly a desire came upon me to look at the sea. The moon was high in the heavens and as we walked up over the field, every thistle, every blade of grass, shone like silver under its light, and the patinated flints and the white scuts of the fleeing rabbits were clearly visible, while above our two heads plovers were wheeling and uttering their cries, sad and wild, into the fresh sea air of the summer night.

I remember clearly the shock of realizing for the first time the ugly fact of death. It was in the End-room at Montacute and on just such an evening. My mother had come to me and had been singing the hymn of which I was most fond, a hymn which described the storm on the Lake of Galilee. The first verse still stays in my memory :

> *A little ship was on the sea,*
> *It was a pleasant sight,*
> *It sailed along so prettily*
> *And all was calm and bright.*

While she was singing I heard the sparrows chirping and rustling in the jasmine as they settled themselves to roost, and this familiar sound, together with the resonant echo of a horse's trot along the Stoke Road, for some reason roused my infant's consciousness to a range beyond the ordinary, and in a single desolate moment my child's mind clearly comprehended the inevitability of one day being separated from my mother. I did not let her know my distress. I did nothing to betray my new knowledge unless it was that I clung to her hand, and, drawing it tightly to me under the counterpane, said my evening prayer with greater fervour :

19

Jesus, tender shepherd, hear me,
Guard Thy little lamb to-night.
Through the darkness be Thou near me,
Keep me safe till morning light.

'God Bless Mother and Father, brothers and sisters, and make Llewelyn a good boy, for Jesus Christ's sake. Amen.'

As I now walked with Alyse towards the sea, over the upland called Tumbledown, I again, as in my babyhood, felt myself fiercely resistant to the harsh ordinance of mortality. We are creatures of the moment, passing shadows ; even the trees exceed us in longevity. To be in possession of fretful thought, and to be short-lived, that is in itself provocative of melancholy ; why, the very elephants who push their way silently through the bamboo forests of Africa are in comparison privileged noblemen of another condition. Every day of all the many decades of their lives they spend in complete firmness of mind. There is only one thing for us to do, to discipline ourselves ungrudgingly to accept the midge-like terms of our existence ; in this way gratitude for what we have got here and now will soon become our dominant emotion. If I look back on the days of my life at home, at school, at Cambridge, everybody I remember seems to be 'lapp'd in lead'—gaping skulls hidden away in rows, underground. Yet consider how each one of these domestic men and women vexed their hearts over the most inconsiderable happenings, the wisest of them too infatuated by the pressure of day-by-day actuality to appreciate the fact that only to be able to look and listen constitutes a sufficient reward. Nothing matters but physical pain and death, all else is experience, enviable enough to the unparticipating folk lying solitary and silent under the churchyard sod.

When we reached the top of the downs the moon was shining clear upon the channel. The summer lights of Portland made a yellow glow in the western horizon and like daggers of gold cast bright reflections far out upon the waves. To the east, towards St. Alban's Head, the sea was white as a shroud under the moon's sovereign power. The fish, with their bland stare, must have been cognizant of her luminosity fathoms deep under the surface of the water. I went up through the gorse and lay down. Very plain I could see the shadows cast by the dizzy lunar escarpments. They were so clear that I could imagine myself gathering up handfuls of moon-mould on any of the great plains, soiling my fingers with the moon's white sand, more silver white than any I had seen beneath the shadows of the palm-trees of the West Indies. And yet it is by the influence of this cosmic clot of floating dust that the oceans of the earth are moved and the bodies of women

inherit their cycles. At that very moment I knew that the
satellite's lustre was being reflected in the eyes of animals
prowling under African cedar-trees ! It was irradiating
their curved claws, giving a lucent outline to the rough
wet tongues of lions as they licked off soft flesh from
blood-smelling bones.

Suppose, I thought, as I lay there by Alyse's side, that John
is right, and that the spirits of men do survive death, and
that we two shall truly be together again at a later-Lammas
tide, recollecting perhaps this very occasion. After all,
the opinions of the greater number of human beings
now living accord with this judgement. As we lay, I could
feel the air of the summer night pass across my back, pass
across my living naked back, which for all it was nothing
but an aggregate of atoms, was yet subject to a tangible
identification from the farthest borders of the universe.
I looked at Alyse's head, it also was actual, each thread of
her fine hair exactly defined. Well enough did I know at
that moment deep in my heart that when once the quick
clay that surrounds our bones is dead it is the end, and
that even François Rabelais was mistaken in supposing
that 'intellectual souls are exempted from Atropos'
scissors.'

4

Father, O Father ! what do we here,
In this Land of unbelief and fear ?
The Land of Dreams is better far
Above the light of the Morning Star.

WILLIAM BLAKE

A S USUAL WE WENT TO BED IN THE OPEN-AIR
revolving shelter which stood near the beehives at
the farther end of the grassy terrace. This shelter
I first acquired when I came back from Africa. At that
time I got leave from Farmer Scutt to establish it in the
garden of the ruined cottage on the top of Jordan Hill to
the east of Weymouth, and each day, by the side of Lod-
moor, that ancient marshland of reeds and rushes and red-
bottomed dykes, I would walk backwards and forwards to
my father's house for breakfast and for supper. During
the years I lived at the White Nose I had this same shelter
put up in a protected dell on the great cliff's edge, and
afterwards, when we first came to Chydyok, in the middle
of a cornfield near the neolithic circle, locally known as the
Pound.

I have always regarded the year 1919, the year I returned

from Africa, as a year of great disappointment. I was thirty-five years old. I had come back determined to write, but nothing I wrote was ever accepted. Up to that time I had believed that one day I would be able to impart a clue, a simple clue that had been mine ever since my boyhood, and yet here I was at the turning-point of my career and nothing done. I had always felt as if I were storing experience for this distant purpose. Even in my schooldays I had entertained such fancies. The same conviction had come strong upon me as I had stood once under the fir-trees of Coker Clump on a wet windy day when I was still an undergraduate, rash and radiant, at Corpus. During the summer with Dittany Stone all had been forgotten, but again in Africa I was aware of this same sense of an outlawed dedication, for I remember, when in danger from a wounded lion, thinking to myself, 'If I am mauled to death now, I shall never have written a word.'

I woke in the small hours of the morning, and got out of the shelter to make water with no kind of suspicion that there was any pad in the straw. I felt supremely happy. In my dreams I had been swimming in a deep tropical ocean and the memory of the blueness of the waves, of the warmth of the day, still bewildered my imagination. From a world of happy shadow sensations I had once more

waked to a world of happy real sensations. The knowledge that I was alive, in the heyday of my life on earth,
with my cradle behind me and my coffin not yet, caused
me to experience as I stood in the cool midnight garden
a tremor of high exhilaration. The soft wandering breath
of the summer night touched my forehead. The moon,
wan as ever, was still high in the heavens. When I got
back into bed I was tempted to wake Alyse, who with
even respirations lay fast asleep. I longed to call her soul
to a living wakefulness just as my soul had been called
back to it. I longed to talk with her and to show her positive incontestable proof of our being alive. I desired, for
instance, that she should look long at the bramble patch
with its motionless blackberry trailers, used, time out of
mind in Dorset, for the binding and belting about of straw
skeps ; I wanted her to share with me the balmy air and
to recognize each one of the sheep-bitten downs stretching
away and away, our bodies still free to range over them.
I did not wake her. I had often indulged such an impulse,
but that night she was sleeping so peacefully that I hesitated, remembering how the Masai had taught me that
if you wake a human being suddenly there is danger that
the truant soul may not have time to come back to
reanimate the body.

I could not have been asleep for more than half an hour
when I found myself for a second time wide awake.

Something was wrong with my chest. I waited for a few seconds lying on my back; the sensation, a horrible bubbling sensation, grew more unmistakable and I knew for certain that I was about to have a hæmorrhage. I could feel that my chest was rapidly filling up with blood. Every time I took a breath my lungs made an alarming gurgling sound that could have been audible fifty yards away, a sound such as one hears sometimes at night on the farther side of a wintry hedge where a poor daft ewe is coughing, her teeth chattering cold from scraping at the rinds of begrimed turnips with quivering underlip. If any ghosts were abroad that night in our garden, drifting like mist over the lavender bush, I am sure they sighed the one to the other, 'There is a living man at the top of the garden and his cough is calling him to the Church-yard-mould where the long coffin-worms batten and crowd.'

Confronted by this sudden unexpected menace to its existence my body cowered back upon itself. For five or ten minutes it was impossible for me to prevent a periodical shivering. I could not keep my legs still, they made the very bed shake, it was as if my several bones were knocking together. Then slowly my mind gathered its own reserves of strength and I could feel my spirit with-drawing itself to some impregnable central 'Castle Keep,' and before the white dawn began to break I was serene once more, knowing that my power was not lost. The bleeding returned at regular intervals of some eight hours. It was not until the late afternoon that I suffered a second attack. It seemed to me likely enough that such violent bleedings would have an ill ending. I could only explain this sudden visitation by thinking that there was at work in my chest some fresh activity resolute to kill. Gradually, however, the conviction grew upon me that I was a victim of the mysterious influence of the sun, that my sun-bathing had given the sun's rays an opportunity to penetrate my skin, and to stir up each disordered cell in the sick centre of my body. During those hot dog-days I had, like Jacob of old, wrestled with my deity, and it was as if with my bare body I had been wrestling with a golden lion : I, a mortal, had been bold to strive with an immortal, and carelessly I had been killed by the splendour of a god.

I found that I felt less helpless when I was supported by a pillow and not lying flat on my two shoulder-blades. In this position, with my legs crossed under me like a Buddha in a garden pagoda, I sat. One strong wish possessed me. I wanted, if I died, to be buried on the open downs, buried in the chalk with my arms and legs flexed after the manner of the men of the old time. I had always recoiled from the prospect of being carried in a customary coffin to the graveyard of the parish church of Chaldon

Herring, that consecrated acre where the dead lie in
rows like fallen dominoes with their arms piously crossed
after the obsequious Christian fashion. To be borne
naked to a grave within a hundred yards of where I lay
seemed no great despite. What had I to fear? The earth
is a good shelter. My senses would be functioning no
longer. My consciousness would have been annihilated,
the particles forming my body would soon enough fall
away to new transformations. For a thousand, for perhaps three thousand years, like the skeletons knaved out of
the sod on Maiden Castle to loll once more for the nonce
in the sunshine, my bones would remain intact. There
would lie my skull, that had so often been merry with
gibes of bawdry, and the gape of whose mouth had so often
been stuffed with bread ; and those same two hands that
had shaken down hazel nuts in Silver Wood, or on lamp-
lit tables turned over the pages of the Bible, of Rabelais, of
Hobbes ; and my feet with which I had paddled in
streams, in hedgerow ditch-streams, or with which I had
in my eager youth come clambering up out of rivers
brim-full to their cuckoo-flower banks. And my mind,
at the very first jump it would be irrevocably destroyed
and the dream of my earth life would have vanished,
vanished as utterly as sea-frit when it lifts from the cliffs
in November. The thought of so dread a forgetting
put me upon a course by which I was able to carry my

illness lightly enough. My friends, who are well aware of my physical timidity—ears flat on my head like any seely Wat—

> *By this, poor Wat, far off upon a hill,*
> *Stands on his hinder legs with listening ear,*
> *To hearken if his foes pursue him still.*

would have been astonished could they have known how little I was incommoded during those days by the close proximity of death. Taking for granted that these were to be the last hours of my life, and stubbornly dismissing all qualms and frights, I resolved to employ myself in bringing back to my mind the story of my first love. I would drive my thoughts out to their memories as a flock of geese might be driven by a punctual goose-herder on to a paddock of clover.

> *In every child of earth*
> *There runs thro' his head from birth*
> *A broken stammered tune,*
> *The fairy-tale of his days.*

I remember my mother once saying to me, ' I can never understand how people can call life short ; if I think of my childhood at Yaxham life seems to me very long '— but, as I lay on my sick-bed meditating upon the days of my youth, my life seemed to have been stolen from me, to have slid by me in a trice, gone, gone, gone all my days before I had had any time to spend them to a sure profit. It was but yesterday, it seemed to me, that I had cried to be allowed to attend the celebrations of Queen Victoria's first Jubilee. They were being held in Lawsell, that broad meadow under Miles Hill, from out of which, when it was put up for hay, I would hear corncrakes calling through the summer evening as I lay awake in the night-nursery. And it seemed but yesterday that, in blazing sunshine, I ran back to the Portugal-laurel when a carriage-and-pair came suddenly down the drive, and I, flying for safety in my white frock ; but yesterday that my sister Marian and my brother Bertie had given me a mug from Miss Sparkes's shop on my fourth birthday, standing all three together at the top of the back passage near the medicine cupboard !

My sister Nelly has been dead now for more than forty years and yet how clearly I remember her teaching me the ' Song of the Shirt ' as I walked by her side on the way to look for linnets' nests in the Battlefield. Her grave-mound may still be seen by the grave-mounds of my father and mother. It has a small white marble cross at its head with the words ' God is love ' upon it. The daisy mound is well cared for to-day, but when my brothers and sisters are dead, who will remember this imaginative child bereft of her life on an April morning so long ago ? Surely her light bones and little skull will be entirely lost among other jumbled bones, she, who had once been the laughing leader of a nursery of children ? Yet in those days, in the days of the early 'nineties, life seemed sufficiently solid, with overworked horses hauling yellow blocks of stone, packed in bracken, down from Ham Hill, with the Phelipses at Montacute House, and Nancy Cooper to be met with in the lanes, and ' Vote for Strachey ' stuck up in revolutionary red upon every wall during election times !

Where now is that life, that life of permanence ? Only a few elderly people remember it. To the younger generation it no longer exists, and before the century is over it will have entirely vanished from the mind of man, vanished as utterly as the leaves of Park Cover which in those days would lie deep enough to top my child's gaiters when, with sturdy strides, I came rustling through them. Yet it was not to the days of my childhood, nor to the days of my boyhood, nor, indeed, to my three riotous years at Cambridge that my mind now reverted. It was to the summer of my twenty-third year, when, during the fleeting weeks of that single summer, I lived through my first experience of intense love. All the poetry in my nature centred itself with sudden passion upon a single girl. For me she was the sun and moon,

the sea, the hills, and the rivers, the cornfields, the hayfields, the plough-lands, and the first stars of nightfall.
Everything that is lovely in nature became illumined by
the thought of her : the garden at dawn, as I saw it looking down from the nursery window on the Round-beds
and the Crescent-bed, populated with cold, diffident
flowers : the meadows by the stream, so hushed in the
night air, heavy with the scents of honeysuckle hedges
and disturbed only by an occasional deep sighing from
one of the ruminating cattle, with weighty body of warm
flesh recumbent upon wet summer grass.

From the moment I had seen her in the church I could
think of nothing else. My whole approach to life was
altered. I no longer cared whether I was to be a poet or
not a poet, I no longer was concerned with the deeper
problems of existence. Unless I could associate what I
saw, heard, tasted, smelt, and touched with her I no longer
gave it attention. What reason was there for me to heed
the waves that broke day and night against the irregular
coasts of the world, to exult in the grass that grew day
and night upon the broad back of the stationary land,
to watch from ancient elbow-bone bridges the flowing
away of rivers, to look up at the crafty midnight stars,
unless such appearances could be made to serve in some
way as poetical settings for this girl of my utter idolatry ?
It seemed to me then, as indeed it seems to me still, that

every inch of her body shone with some mysterious light.
' There was not such a gracious creature born ' ; that she
breathed, that she walked, that she slept to wake again,
was an unending source of wonder to me.

5

An four-and-twenty ladies fair
Will wash and go to kirk,
But well shall ye my true-love ken,
For she wears goud on her skirt.

BALLAD

Y FATHER HAD PROMISED TO OFFICIATE AT A
Sunday evening service in a neighbouring
church and had asked me to go with him.
It was the last day of April. I took my place in the
chancel and after a few perfunctory moments upon my
knees began listlessly to look about me. Suddenly I
saw her sitting in one of the transepts. In my whole life
I never again received so sharp a shock, so convincing
a realization of the swerving movements of destiny. To
me, drowsily imprisoned in an ancient sacerdotal building, in a sacerdotal building smelling of bottom-drawer
Sunday clothes, pontifical vestments, and of God
Almighty, the whole of earth existence became in one
instant transformed with a new radiance. She was
eighteen years old ; her birthday, as she afterwards told
me, had been at Candlemas. As long as a bird sings

before Candlemas she shall greet after it. My heart beat faster and faster. It was as if I had always known her, as if I, in my grass green youth, had recognized my fate as instantaneously as a star falls across the sky on a summer's evening.

> *Hyde ye your beauties, Isoude and Eleyne;*
> *My Lady cometh, that at this may disteyne.*

Presently, when the congregation knelt, I looked at her again through the bars of my fingers.

> *Mine eyes*
> *Were not in fault for she was beautiful.*

Schopenhauer somewhere declares that the first flashing impression that is got of a new face is always the correct impression. I was to see Dittany's face in many moods, but the set image I would hold in anticipation of seeing her, and in retrospect after having been with her, was always as she appeared when for the first time she gave me a look as bright as a summer morning in that dim Somerset church.

The building offered a fitting background for her. There was always something mediæval about Dittany, a mediæval intermingling of childishness and extreme sophistication. And this impression that she really and truly had been born out of due time was strengthened

35

when you saw her eyes that were, whenever her oval face was in repose, of the same narrow level shape that belongs to the eyes of the heavy-gowned ladies to be seen on the illuminated parchment pictures of the old manuscripts. Dittany's eyes would remain aslant like this for hours together during occasions of weariness or dejection, and then would all at once, beyond belief, open wide and wider with an expression of the most blameless candour, should her attention have been startled back to the states of innocent natural happiness that had been common as daisies to her as long as the charmed hours of her childhood had lasted.

> *In the house of the moon where I was born*
> *They fed a silver unicorn*
> *On golden flowers of the sun.*

It was plain that she had nothing to do with the girls of her generation, with the girls of that staid decade before the Great War. Her presence seemed in an odd way to suggest not only the world of mediæval mortals but also the mediæval fairy world. I do not mean the world of the small elves of Shakespeare's fancy, but the world of the mysterious great fays of which in the older ballads we sometimes catch rumours. There exist two words that might be used to describe her, although they have both been so often profaned—the word ' strange,' and the word

'romantic.' She certainly belonged to an age in which
passion and grace were attributes more highly to be
prized than chastity and truth.

Her hair, nor loose, nor tied in formal plat,
Proclaimed in her a careless hand of pride.

It was often possible to see purple shadows in it. Perhaps
its colour was identical with what the Greeks meant by
the word hyacinthine. She wore it loosely looped back
over her temples. The parting was almost always crooked.
How dearly I came to love this little white cringle-crangle
woodland footpath that ran so unevenly across the top of
her beautiful head, like the irregular tracks that the African
natives make through their tangled forests of sunshine and
shadow. But I remember too fast. At present this sel-
couth girl, so rarely fashioned in body and mind, was
kneeling by the side of her mother and father, idling over
her prayer-book with aimless thoughts. Not God above
gets all men's love. There she knelt, a little human lady,
not two decades old yet, her knees resting upon a hassock
with flaps at each end like spaniel's ears, a hassock which
itself rested upon uneven slabs of chill foot-worn Ham
Hill stone, below which, not so very far down under
ground, lay the bones of other girls, whose hair, brown
as November leaves, yellow as corn, or black as the wings
of Hedgecock rooks, although not combed for centuries,

37

still doubtless preserved some sheen, such as I once had noticed in the case of a dead woman whose skeleton had been lying in the dry sand of a catacomb for nearly two thousand years. Dittany's mother was tall, with a proud, well-bred presence. Her father was a stout man with something soldier-like in his bearing.

It was twilight, a calm spring twilight, by the time my father and I began going home. My father always experienced, I think, feelings of relief when he found himself walking away from a church, the service over ! On these occasions he would start down the road at a swinging rate, and then as suddenly slacken his pace, uttering the words ' easy all,' an expression retained from his rowing days at Cambridge, and used now as a conciliatory kind of reproof to any one of his six sons who happened to be with him, and who had been trying to keep up with his longer strides.

It was a cold clear evening, with a primrose light in the sky. The air we breathed was pellucid as a mountain stream and seemed faintly yellow as is sometimes the case in the spring at the time when the first white dust is showing on the roads ; as though the celandines, dandelions, daffodils, and primroses had lightly stained the wandering winds with their happy colours. I could think of nothing but Dittany. I did not then even so much as know her name.

I will gather pears, my lovely one,
To put in thy lap.

I had heard my sister say that some new people called Stone had bought one of the houses in the neighbourhood, and that was all. My feet now went dancing along the road dry-shod as if they were treading on frosty crackling cat-ice. I hardly thought. I only knew that the blood in my body was nimble as wine and that all my bones were leaping with life and that my heart was beating with a new joy, that I was as the god-like son of Odysseus when Athene shed on him ' wondrous grace,' and that I was as a May Lord whose full lips were rounding the mouth of a grass-green horn, blowing for his own brave delight pæan after pæan, and all this because I felt, because I knew I had seen my love.

6

Hark ! hark ! the lark at heaven's gate sings,
And Phoebus 'gins arise,
His steeds to water at those springs
On chaliced flowers that lies ;
And winking Mary-buds begin
To ope their golden eyes ;
With everything that pretty bin,
My lady sweet, arise !
Arise, arise !

WILLIAM SHAKESPEARE

SINCE COMING DOWN FROM CAMBRIDGE I HAD BEEN sleeping in the nursery. This room faced the south and I liked sleeping in it very much. From where I lay I looked directly into the straggling branches of the old acacia, and when I sat up in bed I could see the bough of a deodar tree in the Montacute House drive, which to my childish fancy had always taken to itself on rainy, windy afternoons the wild appearance of a galloping bison.

That Monday morning I woke early. The sun must have only lately risen from behind the distant elm-trees of Vagg Farm. The air that came in through the sash-window was fresh as well-water. There was no longer need for hints and whispers of the approach of spring. There was no reason for further waiting. There could be no mistake now that the spring was present.

> *The fair maid who, the first of May,*
> *Goes to the fields at break of day,*
> *And washes in dew from the hawthorn-tree,*
> *Will ever after handsome be.*

My sister had told me all that I wanted to know about Dittany. Fancy flees upon the wind and from six to seven I lay in my bed planning what I should do. I decided to spend the morning as close to her house as I could get. He needs little advice that is lucky. If possible I would try to see her figure move down the drive or cross the lawn under the great cedar trees or perhaps enter the stone summer-house behind the fish-pool.

With what largess that May morning spread its sunshine over the rambling garden of Montacute Vicarage, penetrating to every flower-bed and patch of grass, or mossy unfrequented cinderpath. I was continually looking out of the window as I dressed. The Portugal-laurel was in full bloom and its white spiral blossoms made the air as odorous to breathe as the zephyrs of a sultry trumpet-flowered tropical glade. Behind the thin little round leaves of the acacia I could hear the tireless tapping of a tree-creeper's bill, and everywhere the well-mown lawn was peopled with parent birds on the look-out for food to carry back to their nestlings—blackbirds, starlings, thrushes, robins, and hedge-sparrows, the last, after their fashion, gravely hopping about with one foot forward— all of the birds scrupulously alert to inspect every inch of the dampened ground, though the shadow they ex- amined should be no more extensive than that cast by a purple hyacinth, drowsy with its own heady fragrance, and drooping over the well-trimmed edge of one or other of the flower-bed borders.

When at last I was out in the garden I found that my father had left his study almost as soon as he had come downstairs and had already been occupied in walking up and down the Terrace-Walk for half an hour. He greeted me with great geniality. Early morning bees were mur- muring in the clumps of arabis that lolled in dense folds over the terrace border stones ; behind the arabis, anemones white, blue, and scarlet, shone out gaily against the dun mould of the flower-bed. The mild spring air was perfumed with the smell of wallflowers in the sun, wallflowers, and the flowering red currant. From some- where in the old lane, on the other side of the white orchards, a cuckoo was calling. I seldom remember to have seen my father in a better temper and his good humour was reflected on his benign good man's countenance. ' This is a fine spring morning,' he kept repeating, and then in a more solemn tone, ' We have much to be thankful for.' The sunshine seemed to affect his whole being. He kept walking up and down the sixty yards of well-trod gravel, all the time rubbing his hands, as was a habit of his when deeply moved. During such moods his features, under the influence of his ecstatic spasms, would entirely alter.

Presently we came to a standstill in front of the fernery at the top-end of the terrace. The apple trees were in their early blossoming and each bough was garlanded with pale petals and rosy buds, the ground between the trees was fair and fresh, ' and every little grass broad itself spreadeth.' A nuthatch was flying to its secure nest in the pig-apple tree and a redstart to its soft nursery in the hollow of another tree, a tree so slanting that its trunk bent at an angle of scarce six foot from the ground. A sulphur butterfly came fluttering towards us with no set intention in its wavering aerial passage, and with its minute feckless head, virgin of all thought save the pretty task of sipping nectar from warm bright petals or the outspreading of its wings in the sun in preparation for dancing flights with a sunbeam love, flights that would end at last, curling tail to curling tail, in a motionless ecstasy daintier in operation than the flicker of a child's eyelash. The tabby cat also made his appearance, sauntering

43

up from the corner near the kitchen-garden path, solitary, self-centred, luxuriously gratified by the blissful sensation of heat penetrating to his skin through an oilless tabby fur. He trod delicately, lifting his feline pads with careful precision over the gravel, every pebble of which shone like a separate nugget of purest gold. It could hardly be doubted that his indolent parading was prompted by an impulse of life-destructive malice. Excitedly scream-ing above him were the newly-arrived swallows, cutting the sky between the sycamore and the thatched roof of the summer-house with arrow-sharp flights, unmindful of grief.

Spread out above us to the north, to the south, to the east, and to the west, was the wide ceiling of a summer sky of a blue as startling in colour as the hedge-sparrow's eggs in the box-hedge, a sky clear and buoyant, and hollow, and quivering with sunshine—a blue heaven above a green earth, above the land of the living ! Sud-denly my father broke the silence that had fallen between us, broke it with words that strangely affected me, for he was a man of great reserve and it was only under the strongest stress that he would ever reveal religious emotion. 'Praise Father, Son, and Holy Ghost !'

In the dining-room, before the servants came in, there was the same feeling of elation. My mother's face was illumined, the tired lines on her high forehead were less apparent and her tragic deep-set brown eyes brimmed with an unwonted eagerness. I suppose a fine morning in the month of May provokes a deeper and more universal response in the hearts of creatures than almost any happening in nature, unless it be rain after a drought. On the topmost branch of the feathery larch tree the glossy cock blackbird with golden bill sang with never-ending passion to his mate below in the laurustinus.

> *When the hen-bird's wing doth rest*
> *Quiet on her mossy nest.*

The servants appeared at last and sat in order on the chairs by the long mahogany sideboard, in one cupboard of which was kept sherry for visitors, and in the other a portable communion service used by my father when visiting the sick. ' Teach us who survive in this and other daily spectacles of mortality, to see how frail and uncertain our own condition is . . . For man that is born of woman hath but a shadow of time to live.' My father now read a chapter from the Bible, his long legs stretched out under the table. We then all knelt down to listen to his extemporary prayers, prayers expressed in the firm spacious language of the English liturgy, prayers invoking God's providence to be over us all in our ' goings out and comings in.'

And I, while I noted the familiar scratches and blemishes

45

on the leather covering of the chair against which I knelt,
and admired the shaft of sunlight, which, lying along the
carpet like a spear, almost penetrated to the crack under the
door, and was conscious of the garden birds outside flashing by the tall French windows, could hardly wait for the
final blessing. How patriarchal a breakfast at Montacute
Vicarage could be with my father cutting the wheaten
bread, ' bread such as is usual to be eaten ; but the best
and purest wheat bread that conveniently can be gotten,'
and helping his children generously to buttercup-yellow
butter, and my mother at the end of the table pouring out
the tea, and all of us hungry and unaware of death.

When breakfast was over like a very May-fool I rushed
away. I was not long in reaching Stoke Wood. There
were places where the wood was grown so thick with
fir trees that as children we used to pretend, when the
ground was frozen or it had snowed, that we were passing
through a Russian, wolf-haunted forest. Two sentinel
jays now began to scream at me, for here as elsewhere all
creatures were clamorous with affirmations of life on such
a morning. I reached the great white-rinded beech tree
which, like some memorable trunk in the forest of Arden,
a tree huge of girth, was fretted with the names of generations of village lovers from Stoke and Montacute. The
ground of the woodland was thick carpeted with dog's
mercury, no bare places of earth were left exposed, all was

covered over with the males and females of the odd dioecious plant, they spread far and wide, the ovary of each feminine pistil aptly accessible to the golden dust-clouds of their desire, indeed, idly languishing for fertilization, deliciously floating down upon them at every ground-breath of the breeze. I was standing looking at this unprofitable harvest streaked and splashed with sunlight when suddenly I realized that somebody was coming down the sloping path opposite. It was Dittany Stone !

See where she comes apparell'd like the spring.

She held in her hand a broad summer hat and she walked over the ruts with slow, dreaming steps as though the day held her also under a kind of trance. The luck of having met her was so remarkable to me that I got an odd feeling that some love deity had interfered for our advantage. Indeed, I have in my life often observed that lovers possess a strange power of persuading accidental meetings to take place, much in the same manner as a female moth is able to conjure her love to her however wrapped in velvet darkness a garden may be.

Herrick, I think, had the same fancy when he wrote :

So silently they one to th' other come,
As colours steale into the Peare or Plum,
And Aire-like, leave no pression to be seen,
Where e're they met, or parting place has been.

47

I did not know what to do. When we were still a few yards apart she looked up. I hesitated for a moment in front of her. She also paused. My heart was beating so fast I felt as if I could not speak. 'Didn't I see you in church yesterday?' I said a little awkwardly. She did not seem in the least embarrassed. She stood regarding me with wide-open eyes. There was something about her manner that at once relieved us of the teasing responsibilities of adult intercourse. She told me afterwards that she thought this peculiar immunity from the various pressures that the conventional world exercise over most of us came from her being an only child and from her having spent so much time in her own dream world, more real than reality.

Nimue the Enchantress came
To visit Merlin. Did I know
How the deep enchantments go?
With Merlin I am sleeping yet;
And time and loss are shut away
From the garden where all suns have set.

Just as to an owl warming its five wits in the tower of East Chaldon Church our day is its night, and our night its day, so to Dittany our real world was her shadow-world and our shadow-world was her actual world. She would drift through her life, drift and drift, her mind clouded

48

with indolent day-dreams, and upon occasions her face, so sensitive and pale, would appear like the face of the drowned girl by the milldams of Binnorie. I have often thought that it was her extreme sensitiveness that made her intellectually so remarkable. Because of the sheltered life she had lived the brutalities of the world so outraged her feelings that, like Lady Jane Grey, she had come to rely upon her mind for her happiness more than most of us do. 'I wis all their sport in the Park is but a shadow to that Pleasure that I find in Plato.'

In spite of her extreme youth she had in some ways the emancipated intelligence of a far older woman, of a woman to whom it is natural never to reveal what she is thinking except under conditions of the severest provocation. 'Men byhove to take hede of maydens : for they ben hote and tendre of complexion ; smale, pliaunt and fayre of disposicion of body ; shamfaste, ferdefull and mery touchynge the affeccion of the mynde.' I saw from the first that she was a most unusual girl to come upon. She already knew much poetry. She never forgot any word she had read or any word she heard spoken, and yet she had the quality of extreme innocence too, an authentic and innate innocence of mind and spirit that no dealings with man could corrupt.

I was utterly at a loss what to say to her, how to delay her. Then suddenly, without premeditation, the words

49

came. 'Let me show you some fox-holes.' At the
simplicity of this unexpected overture she gave a free
conspiring laugh, arching her eyebrows, a trick of hers
when surprised and when she felt that any particular
situation was approaching the margin of her own unpredictable world of dreams.

7

Yea, many there be that have run out of their wits
for women, and become servants for their sake,

ANCIENT WISDOM

I LED HER UP OVER THE DOG'S MERCURY. I TOO FELT AS
if I had escaped out of the time I knew and was really
conducting a little princess away from her proper path
and up the side of a great forest where I might presently
observe in the soft mould the tracks left by a wild boar or
see against the leaves large and long, the shining forked
head of a standing stag. She followed me in silence
through the chequered sunlight, lifting away swaying
branches with her hands and stepping over the fallen tree
trunks. I thought how all the other girls I knew would
have destroyed the charm of those treasured moments, preg-
nant with future happenings, by a flow of self-conscious
chatter to cover their embarrassment. She was one to
whom out-of-ordinary situations were ordinary. Herself
created them, and she accepted them as the natural background to *her* world. Never was anybody less implicated
in the modes of her period. Never was there anybody
so utterly untouched by prevailing beliefs and prejudices.

We came to the wall that ran right across Hedgecock, dividing the Chaffey property from the Phelips property, and I helped her over it. Arrows of sunlight darted and flickered through the spruce firs, illuminating the mossed stones, and the grass, and hart's-tongues, and the patches of bare woodland soil under the trees. Once over the wall I led her to the place where I knew the foxes had their holes at the crest of one of the steepest slopes. The entrances to these earths were often so large that it would easily have been possible for a boy to crawl down them. ' Isn't this a lovely home for a fox to have ? ' I said, looking appreciatively about me. ' Think of him,' and I tried to picture to her some old dog fox coming back through the dewy fields from Betsy's orchard, his pointed ears still tingling with the clamour of the poultry he had terrified. Fie upon hens, quoth the fox. ' Think of him coming over the place where the wall is broken in Bride's Mead with the smell of chicken feathers still hanging about the red hairs of his narrow chin and yet his belly hungry ! ' I told her too how he would saunter out of his hole in the late autumn evening, at the hour when the rooks are returning, with his sly mask looking cunningly about, indifferent utterly to the poetry of the twilight, scratching at the thick scruff of his neck with impatient hind-foot, his bushy tail resting upon the clay.

Dittany, while I was talking, had sat down on the dry

pine-needles to the right of the platform that was before the beast's dwelling. Her hat was at her side and her hands were held together on her lap. She had been listening to my words with silent attention. Reclining there, she seemed a very bank of summer flowers. If I had dared I would have taken her into my arms and given her a hundred kisses. The shadow that her hair made across her temple seemed to me the fairest thing I had ever seen, like the shadow of a vernal grass upon the white flesh of a rounded mushroom. Her hands too were so delicate and her fingers as little as bobbins. Indeed, standing there on the platform of deep burrowed-out loam, marked so conspicuously by fox-pads, I could hardly bear to think of her body in all its beauty so near to me, her long small arms with ' phœnix-down ' in each sheltered cup, and with veins blue as the flax flower, wandering down the inside of her forearm as it were like azure streams gently meandering across a daisy lea ; her breasts, even yet not fully formed, her young waist ! In truth but to think of one dainty limb leading to another more dainty limb was enough to set me trembling.

' Let me see if I can crawl down,' she exclaimed, and careless of her pretty frock, she rapidly approached the foxhole on hands and knees. I was half afraid that she would presently leave me gazing hour after hour at a dull hedgecock burrow, anxiously bereft in a wide-awake rational world where the very existence of Dittany Stone could scarcely be conceived.

She did go down the hole till I could only see the heels of her shoes and then she caught her hair in an overhanging root, which showering dry earth down upon her, made her quickly back out again. ' Robert Herrick,' she said, as she shook the crumbs of dry soil from her hair, ' used to play at a Christmas game called " Fox-in-hole," I wonder what sort of game it was. . . . It is strange to think,' she went on, ' that the holes of foxes were so well known to Jesus that they came naturally to his mind when he wanted to give an example of a safe hiding-place.' After a while we rose and slowly went out of the wood, walking by the side of the wall. I was happy. I held her hand. She did not demur.

Our direction led us down through the trees to a foot-path which wound its way to the valley over two fields thick-grown with spring corn, and separated the one from the other by an old-fashioned stile between two trees.

> *Butterflies are white and blue*
> *In this field we wander through.*
> *Suffer me to take your hand,*
> *Death comes in a day or two.*

This foot-path-way brought us eventually to a broad grassy drove which is as deserted and lovely a lane as

ever I have walked along, especially during the hay-
making weeks of the high summer, when both of its
hedges would be heavily wreathed with 'comely ruddy
dog-roses.' By the side of this grass-floored, bird-haunted
thoroughfare there stood a ruined cottage. It was a place
I liked to come to and I now conducted Dittany into the
roofless dwelling. To enter we had to go up some five
or six steps of Ham Hill stone, round steps that in their
centre had been worn away by the iron-shod farm-boots
of generations of Somerset labourers and by the tough
shoe-leather of their children. The gaping chimney still
showed black from hearth-fires that must have been
extinguished for already half a century. Nettles and bur-
docks and brambles flourished near the walls of the old
room, while every flagstone with which the floor had
been paved was fringed with knot-grass. As we came in,
a thrush flew out of an elder-tree whose branches
obstructed the entrance to what once no doubt had served
as a kitchen. I found the bird's nest and showed it to
Dittany. It contained five eggs. Half-fearfully, as
though nervous of doing a mischief, she touched them,
hen-warm, ink-dotted, and of so peerless a blue. Together we admired the nest's construction, its concave
interior so firmly pasted with clay, smooth-moulded by
devoted breast and beak. No wonder, we thought, the
gypsies cherish the nests of thrushes as receptacles for the

milk they steal from midnight cattle, using them as handy porridge bowls for fire-hugging urchins. When I was alone with Dittany, life's usual dreary domino would instantaneously fall away and I would find myself walking upon magical mud, while every crooked twig in the hedge, and every flying feather in the air would be limned against a glancing infinite wherein the humblest material object was implicit with a vast yet warrantable reality, across the solid margins of which we would pass together, blithe of step and with eyes undeluded, in a sustained trance of inexplicable happiness. I now found a dry place for Dittany to sit down on and myself rested near the hearthstone. The smell of sun-warmed nettle leaves was everywhere. With hands clasped about her knees she remained for several minutes perfectly motionless. Through the door she could see a distant slope of Ham Hill, a slope parrot-green against the squared fragment of the cloudless May-day sky ! How many coffined dead men and coffined dead women must have been carried out through that door, and how many children had first seen the glory of light from those yellow steps, now nothing more than a convenient vantage-place for water-wagtails, or for some fur-washing hedge-rat seated here in the undisturbed hour of the sun-rising, its selected platform growing, moment by moment, warmer under its tail, until such a time as the over-slept dairyman's man

would come striding down the drong, breeches un-
buttoned and boots unlaced, intent upon rousing his large
beasts from their several islands set in seas of sparkling
dew.

Dittany looked even more lovely to me now than she
had done in Stoke Wood. Her head so pale, so poetical,
seemed to appease in some deep way all the secret yearn-
ings of my heart. In her present mood she appeared to
be a creature built up of the thinnest and most immaterial
of all God's atomies, fair as the evening planet I once saw
shining suddenly out above the feathered rushes and
narrow willow leaves of the tangled Bagnel withy-bed ;
fair as a sunset rainbow arching an unmown meadow,
hushed and at peace after a day of slanting rain and gusty
cuckoo cries ; as full of mystery as the moonlight ripples
on a village well, soft-matted with moss and penny-worts,
a watery enchanted vision unperceived by any living
eyes save those of questing moths or of the staring owl with
dangling pounces sailing silently by the tall children-
deserted hedges of a churchyard lane. And yet it was
Dittany's supreme gift that this ethereal quality of hers
was always sib to the earth and to all that was natural and
of the earth. She might appear to be composed only of
the lighter elements, an image formed out of snow, out
of dew, out of tears, but all the time she was tormentingly
tangible, audible, visible, a girl enclosed in a dreaming

case of tremulous sensibility capable of quivering and quivering again at the faintest touch.

She broke the silence at last. 'Listen to that chiff-chaff,' she said. At her words the grassy lane outside seemed suddenly to be chiming from end to end with the shy little bird's reiterated summer utterance, Chiff-chaff ! chiff-chaff ! chiff-chaff ! 'It's ticking away a different sort of time from the world's time,' Dittany remarked. 'It's the time that is always over the hedge, always beyond each gatepost, always on the other side of the next hill !'

8

*Fear not the sentence of death ; remember them that
have been before thee and that come after ; for this is the
sentence of the Lord over all flesh.*

ANCIENT WISDOM

MY MIND HAD SO COMPLETELY FLOWN AWAY THAT
it came back to a consciousness of my predica-
ment on Chaldon Down listlessly, almost with
indifference. It was evening and I was coughing again
and my sister Gertrude was holding the vase up to my
lips. How much blood has a man in his body ? How
could I possibly hope to stop that flow ? With what wad
could I propose to dress the inside of my chest ? I could
not even tell whether the wound was behind my right
shoulder or behind my right pap. I could feel my breathing impeded, and then would have to cough, whether I
liked it or not.

Yet this respite that my memories had given me during
the long day had supplied me with a kind of reserve of
strength. Before the darkness fell this fresh attack had
stopped, and I was able, lying back upon my pillows, to
look out on the downs again with a tranquil mind ; and
as the partridges began to call, and the echoes of human

59

revelry came to me from the holiday camp in the direction
of Lulworth, and the stars appeared one by one, I knew
that my spirit had force in it for what was to come. In
truth so much refreshment had my mind won from its
recollections, from its knowledge of such stored-away
harvests of past happiness, that it was now easy to regard
death with more philosophy. Epicurus had never tired
of teaching that if pain is intense it is soon over and if it
is prolonged and not intense then it allows room for some
degree of conscious pleasure. For which of the horizontal
chrysalises of mortal dust, lying beneath the footworn
floor of Salisbury Cathedral, would not eagerly snatch at
any evening of life, though such an evening were to
include the dread hour of their own deaths?—Better
to be dying, they would say, than dead, better any condition that would allow us once more to look upon
the light of the afternoon sun on the glinting glass of the
manor's mullioned window, or falling across the wall of
a garden dove-cot, grey with lichen and weather-age.

I knew I would have to revive in my memory many
days of that far-off summer if my body was to be released
from its distress. If I tried to recapture what happened in
too exact a sequence, as indeed I could have done if I
had sent someone to fetch my private diary for that year,
then I became confused and troubled and very soon I
would lose my enfranchisement and begin once more

worrying about the issue of the illness, or even about some temporary sensation in my lungs that might presage fresh misery. If, however, I could go over in my mind the happiest walks I had had with Dittany, our happiest meetings, I found I could put myself under so powerful a glamour that I would forget where I was and what was happening to me, could, in fact, make believe the distant summer to be more real than the present one. I had often heard my brother John praise the power of the mind, but it was not till this illness that I understood the meaning of his lifelong confidence. Now I was willing at last to give the mind, the ratio of the five senses, its due. In a crisis of the kind that I was passing through, the body too easily behaves like a granary cat. It relies upon fear for its preservation. My body during those days was ready, at a moment's notice, to be seized by panic. Once when we spent a winter at Steepletop in the Berkshire mountains of New York State with Edna St. Vincent Millay, I was troubled with deafness and went into Chatham to have my ears syringed. The country doctor, dressed in his blue serge suit smelling of stale cigar smoke, tried to probe at the wax with a stick wrapped about with cotton-wool. I used all my will-power to keep still, but no sooner did I feel this sensation of probing than I would jerk away just as a loose-box horse will do when, under the hands of a veterinary surgeon, it feels any portion of its live flesh menaced. During this illness I knew that my body was subject to the same kind of irrational physical responses. When my tongue told me I had coughed up a substance *thicker than blood*, my body wanted to whimper, to look wildly about, crying out for some way of escape. In truth it seemed to me that my body began to suspect its own death and from sheer fright was ready to expire. The mind, I discovered, acted the part of a competent general. It shouldered the responsibility, restored confidence to the panic senses, and with firm understanding completely intimidated Fear so that it slunk out of the way ashamed and discredited. The hour of death is no hour for revolutions.

9

Too weak the wit, too slender is the brain,
That means to mark the power and worth of love ;
Not one that lives, except he hap to prove,
Can tell the sweet, or tell the secret pain.

ROBERT GREENE

AFTER THAT FIRST MORNING I MET DITTANY EVERY day in the wood. Once we walked to Ham Hill and I showed her the chasm between the two unused ivy-covered quarries that as boys we used to leap, but I did not jump it as she became frightened climbing along the slippery bank. She was not happy when on Ham Hill : it was, with its short turf, its thyme and eyebright, too open for her, too much under the dominion of the sun. When whins are out of bloom, kissing is out of fashion. She favoured the gorse-bush alleys in the sloping field which my mother had named the Cathedral, having noted the elevated habit of the trees that grew there, with branches lifted high above the spreading primrose-beds by trunks smooth, powerful, and perpendicular as pillars. Under these trees, in hidden fastnesses of furzen, we would find inaccessible rabbit lawns entirely to our pleasure. In such places I could wait for hours looking into her soft eyes where I was ' mirror'd small in paradise ' ; while the linnets, rosy-feathered, sang fragmentary madrigals, now from this thick-set thorny spray, and now from that.

> *The chuckling linnet, its five young unborn,*
> *To sing for thee.*

To Ham Hill she much preferred the fragmentary earth-works, mossy and cool, or the shady glens, or the sunny warren-dips sequestered behind high forest trees—silent places in the deeper recesses of Stoke Wood, where it used locally to be said fugitives from the Battle of Sedgemoor had hid themselves, for months together, to escape the bloody wrath of Judge Jeffreys. From Ham Stone to Dogtrap Lea a squirrel may leap from tree to tree. How ravishing she looked in such retreats, where lights came fitfully down upon her bare arms through an awning of green confederate leaves, as if she were in very truth the milk-white hind.

> *But be sure ye touch not the milk-white hynde,*
> *For she is o' the woman-kind.*

I would return for lunch, and, after, would sit in the Terrace-Walk and my mother would presently come and read to me with a brown Shetland shawl about her head and shoulders. I remember that she read to me that summer the poems of Walt Whitman, the poems of Thomas Hardy, *The Confessions of Rousseau*, *Tom Jones*, and the *Autobiography of Benvenuto Cellini*. She would sit by my side on a stiff garden chair, and I would give but half my attention to the cadence of her gentle voice, and for the rest my mind would be going over and over what had happened in the morning, recalling the frock Dittany had worn, recalling her sweet ways, her varying expressions, the words she had spoken.

> *He might not in house, field, or garden stir,*
> *But her full shape would all his seeing fill.*

Dittany ! The very syllables of the name had for me a peculiar charm. I had learned all I could about the old medicinal herb. The leaves of the herb dittany (*dictamnus*) are pinnate in form and of a habit feathery soft, its flowers being white. In summer weather this exceptional plant is often enveloped in a mist, a mist of the blue colour of the smoke of a wood fire and of so igneous an endowment as to be set alight should a flame be carried to it. Botanists explain this mysterious property from the fact that the leaves and stems of the plant are decorated with innumerable hairy glands which in Dog-day sunshine exhale, moment by moment, an æthereal vapour, a vapour which, like a sort of veil of Isis, affords an airy covering for this

65

most sensitive and most singular hedgerow wort. I discovered too that the ancients were by no means ignorant of some of the strange qualities possessed by this weed, for in the *Encyclopædia* of Bartholomew Anglicus, which used to stand next to Young's *Night Thoughts* in the spare-room, I came upon the following remarks : 'It is said that a hind taught first the virtue of dictamnus, for she eateth this herb that she may calve easlier and sooner ; and if she be hurt with an arrow she seeketh this herb and eateth it, which putteth the iron out of the wound.'

Presently my reveries would be disturbed by the voices of the turkeys from the orchard field belonging to Sam Hodder on the other side of the lane—gobble, gobble, gobble they would go, and once more gobble, gobble, gobble—and listening to their farmyard clutter I would come to be aware of how stationary those summer afternoons could be in the process of time moving no faster than the standstill shadow that the flowering elder-hedge made upon the orchard grass. Then at last I would see 'The Stunner' come sauntering up from behind the summer-house holly tree, pipe in mouth, and bowler hat, turned green with age, tilted sideways on his head, and the cows, red of hide and in good case, would move slowly away beneath the apple trees for their milking, their hairy ambling legs struck again and again by the tiny clubs of the taller buttercups. Then Mary Hockey would appear from the kitchen-garden path carrying my afternoon glass of milk on the very same silver salver that in the division of my father's property I later inherited. The glass of milk, milk from the udders of these orchard cows, had been standing all the morning in the larder, securely protected from flies, and was often so rich and thick that the first few mouthfuls I took would be of pure cream.

Dittany and I planned one day to meet by the great beech tree and walk from there through Dogtrap and across the Battlefield to Norton Covert. I wanted to show her a spring that I knew, a spring to which it was rumoured the fairies brought their cradle changelings from Bagnel, from Park Plane, from Norton, and from Cheselborough. It was a pool, deep-matted with moss and banded about with roots like snakes.

The morning we selected for the expedition was cloudless. I arrived at our trysting tree and waited. As always I began to dread that she might not be coming, that her heart might misgive her.

> For if I gang to the Broomfield Hill,
> My maidenhood is gone ;
> And if I chance to stay at hame,
> My love will ca' me mansworn.

I never failed to feel on such occasions that for those few scattered hours with her I would make any sacrifice. If only I could see her appear between the familiar guardian trunks ! The value of the current time, which alone was sure of her in the sunshine, seemed infinitely greater than any problematic future good. An antic ancestral prophet, wise in counsel, kept crying to me from somewhere in earth, air, or water :

Yesterday returneth not ;
Perchance to-morrow cometh not;
There is to-day ; misuse it not.

I ran to meet her. How my whole breathless being danced at seeing her again. When I reached her I threw my arms about her and kissed her many times. She flushed at my ardour. I never had seen her looking more lovely. We began walking up the slight incline that separated us from the great forest beech ;—' Oh ! I was so afraid you weren't coming,' I exclaimed. ' I thought something had prevented you, your mother perhaps.' She caught a certain nervousness in my voice conveying my apprehension lest sooner or later her mother might really interfere, for scarcely had we taken a few steps together than she began mockingly to repeat :

' *My father is the nightingale*
Who sings within the bosky dale
On the tallest tree.

68

The mermaiden my mother is,
She who sings her melodies
In the deep salt sea.'

And then just as suddenly grew grave. 'You need not
fear,' she said, 'my mother would never prevent me,
she always lets me do what I want to do, and anyhow
she knows we meet and doesn't mind.'

We arrived at last at the tall white wooden gate opening
into the woodland cart-track that runs round the foot of
Hedgecock. It was still early in the morning and the track
was so shadowed, with laurels on the left and with the
trees of the wood on the right, that the dew had not dried.
Dittany got her shoes and stockings drenched with the
long grass and purple water-mint over which we trod.
'How lovely it is,' she said, looking up the green lonely
thoroughfare. 'It's as though it was all under a spell
and we were walking in the land of Shea !—How still
the lane is ! The butterflies are the only creatures that
can move.' We stood side by side, gazing before us along
that green roadway, rank, luxuriant, and magical. I
can still in my mind's eye evoke it—the bracken, already
ladle tall, the pink campions above and the blue-bells
below, and the sunshine slanting down upon wavering
marbled-whites, whose soft bodies were invisible under
fluttering wings. I threw myself on my knees before

her, and as I looked up at her I remember feeling as if this homely drong, familiar to me since my infancy, had been transformed to a royal path in some greenwood, vert and eldritch, of the Sely Court.

As I walked a little ahead of her, beating down the brambles that trailed over the cart-track, and pushing back the overhanging bracken lest their wet fronds should spoil the freshness of her summer frock, made out of white linen, I told her how I remembered coming here with my brother John and my Aunt Dora and how I ran before them, a little boy, on just such a summer morning, and how I kept beating off the heads of the pink campions with the stick of the wooden hoop that I carried, and how John had called to me, and, because I had taken no notice, had hastened after me, and held me in his arms, and said, 'Llewelyn, you must never, never do that again, never in your whole life—for you must not forget that every tree, every leaf, every flower is alive *as we are alive* and it is only very stupid or very wicked people who can be indifferent to the destruction of their earth companions.' I had never forgotten his words because he had looked at me so very earnestly with his small green-grey tabby-cat eyes. 'It is best,' he said, 'never even to pick flowers ; but you must at any rate never injure them wantonly as you were doing just then.'

Dittany listened eagerly. 'I have always felt like that,'

she said, 'especially when I sleep in the garden, and each one of them seems like a different, separate person.' She begged me to tell her more about my brother. We had reached the place where the road turned to encircle the southern side of Hedgecock and led up to the woodland avenue known as the Beeches. In a few words I tried to give her some conception of my eldest brother, named after John the Baptist, tried to describe his appearance, his low-browed, primordial, soothsayer's skull and his long-fingered hands, thin as autumn leaves, the hands of a very old man, and yet with the gripping power of a demon, and I told her how tall and lean and stooping was the body that housed so mighty a spirit.

At the turn of the avenue we stopped at the foot of the corner beech. No tree in the whole wood was so old or so large as this tree. Dittany had made her shoes so muddy coming up the lane that I gathered a tuft of grass and tried to clean them. She didn't want me to do this for her. She tried to snatch the grass away from me and doing so she got her hands covered with black leaf-mould mud. 'Come,' I cried, 'I will show you a basin where you can wash them,' and I led her round the great trunk of the beech to where two protruding roots had formed a stoup of woodland water. Often as a child I had left the side of Miss Beales to run to examine the cider-coloured liquid in this wooden bowl. 'I will wash your body, Dittany, in the water of the wild rain.' I took her meek hands in mine and dipped them deep into the tree trunk's hollow. 'How lovely!' she exclaimed, and I was delighted by the delight she experienced as she felt the lukewarm water upon her thumbs and upon each of her four fingers. She was entranced by the little catch-basin, made all of wood and surrounded by its tod of softest moss. 'Do the birds come here to drink?' she asked, 'white-throats, and chaffinches, and long-tailed tits?' I dried her hands with my handkerchief. Her little finger was so small that I am sure it could have reached to the end of any of the round holes made by the mason-bees in the sun-hot wall of the East Garden of Montacute House, holes that used to astonish me when we took our nursery walks through the Park, on sunny autumn mornings, to pick up the sycamore leaves which our nurse Emily had taught us to value for the variation of their colour.

Oh! how wonderful it all seemed to me that day. What rapture, to be alive with Dittany, a thousand leaves spreading open to the air about her, and the small birds darting over the meadows below us, and the blackbirds and thrushes singing, and the grey battlements of the Abbey visible as we walked forward under the great trees!

We crossed the waste land called Dogtrap, but before we went through the gate into the Battlefield I took her to the Wishing-Stone that is under the beeches above Forster's Gully. I let her stand first upon the stone. With a secret joy I saw her so seriously silent upon this wizard stone of the walks of my childhood. ' All ignorant that soul that sees thee without wonder.' Her eyes were fast shut. ' I think this is really and truly a place of mystery,' she said at last, when she stepped away to make room for me. ' What a sombre lane ! ' I did not answer. In my turn I was occupied with projecting my very individual and pertinent wish into the air about us.

> For your grace, lady,
> Lovely and white,
> My heart leaps up
> By day, by night.

When I had made my simple invocation I explained to her that the road going up to Ham Hill was the old coach-road to Exeter, and that Forster's Gully was so called because a highwayman of that name had been caught here and hung up in an iron cage to starve to death, and that there were old people in Montacute whose grandparents remembered hearing of the man's cries, ' Forster's starvin' ! Forster's starvin' ! ' ' It is said,' I told her,

73

' that a woman got leave from the guard to speak to the prisoner and pushed a couple of tallow candles through the bars of his hanging prison for him to eat.' I wished I had not repeated to her the old hearsay. Dittany had an extraordinary capacity for imaginative sympathy and could never bear to be told of cruelty, even though it might have happened centuries ago. She shrank from pain in all its forms. Once I noticed a spider eating a struggling house-fly at the top of a dim dusty window. I stood upon the window-seat to observe more narrowly what was taking place, calling to Dittany to do the same. When I looked round, she was pale as a ghost. I used to fancy sometimes that her body was covered by only one skin instead of the seven that the rest of us carry, a skin as white as a lily and of a texture as tender.

We now went through the five-barred gate on the other side of the road. We skirted the Battlefield, keeping to the sheep-tracks that ran under the top hedge. The mouths of each of the sandy rabbit-holes shone yellow bright in the morning sunshine. The field's real name was Witcombe. It was my brother John who had named it the Battlefield because it was formed with two steep slopes rising opposite to each other, suggesting to his imagination the topography of the old-fashioned pictures of battles that our uncle Littleton had painted on large sheets of drawing-paper, and which had remained in my father's album since the Stalbridge days, the French charging down on one side and the English charging down on the other side, with the ugly iron cannons of the Napoleonic period shooting balls over the heads of the two combatants, and over their flags bright-coloured as popinjays. At the bottom of the opposing slopes was a level valley in which Dr. Hensleigh Walter, the local antiquarian, used to tell me there had once stood the village of Witcombe, abandoned at the time of the Black Death and never reinhabited. I told Dittany about this forgotten village, and from where we had sat down, elbows on knees, we could distinguish the shadowy outlines of the foundations of its cabins under the grass. The morning was unequalled. I could hear the yaffle, laughing and calling in Horses' Covert—'What fools, what fools you mortals be !' From the mild pastoral slope on which we were resting I could see growing in the grass, where the cottages had used to stand, clusters of yellow flowers. I knew what they were, wild daffodils ! They had always grown here, possibly descended from the fourteenth century garden flowers, very short in the stalk now and yet carrying bravely enough their cold single trumpets. Dittany noticed another vegetable growth of a darker foliage and I explained to her that this was hellebore, also probably brought here by those old peasants who had sat

75

by wood fires in mud-and-wattle huts discussing battles in France and the prowess of their Black Prince, as they whittled away at their long bows of church-yard yew. England were but a fling save for the crooked stick and the grey-goose wing.

IO

Surely she was the most beautiful woman that ever water washed.

BALLAD

WE WENT THROUGH THE LITTLE GATE INTO THE wild bracken-grown ground above Norton Covert. It is a rough acreage, bordered by an earthwork that leads away to Ham Hill. Everywhere the hawthorn trees were in blossom. I had never seen them more beautiful nor the turreted bracken so tall or of so tender a green. She was now a little in front of me and I observed her distinctive walk as she adventured through the ferns. She did not dance or trip along lightly as other girls. Her advance possessed no hint of resolution in it. On all occasions, whether she was going through field or forest, along sheep-walk, or over cow-pasture, it seemed that her course might be diverted by a bramble, by a breath ! We climbed through a shard in the hedge into the wood. I wanted to discover a secret place and soon was successful. In the heart of the wood a great tree had fallen and by balancing along its prostrate trunk we were able to reach a secluded patch of green ground surrounded by blackberry-bushes and hazel-nut trees. It was here that I made her a bed. As if she guessed what was in my mind she took her hat off and hung it with shy deliberation upon a branch of the fallen tree. It happeth in one hour what happeth not in seven years. I was trembling.

> *These blue vein'd violets whereon we lean*
> *Never can blab, nor know not what we mean.*

In silence, without speaking a word, we drew together. Her cheeks were flushed.

My love for her, my desire for her, could never be appeased. My passion for her was so inordinate that I saw her beauty as it were with the vision of a God, with the eyeballs of Siva. Although she was unwilling to concede the last union, to be fast joined, that is to say, as fell to flesh and as hardly to be separated, our loving was passionately intemperate. Every inch of her body shone for me like the radiant skin of Aphrodite when she lay entangled—a shining silver-white dace of a lady—in her goodman's meshed net of gaudy brass.

> *Take care, take care ;*
> *If anyone look,*
> *If anyone stare,*
>   *Tell it me !*
> *In the leafy thickets over there ;*
> *Beware, beware*
> *If anyone stare !—*

'Look at that dragon-fly sitting guard over me so faith-fully,' she cried once. The great horse-stinger, with its net-veined glittering wings, had settled on a leaf above us and there sat with globular compound eyes regarding Dittany's disordered frock and scattered looks. 'For all his rude staring he is a dragon that hasn't guarded me so very well,' she complained. The place where we were lying smelt of the summer wood, of newly burgeoning leaves, of inconspicuous flowers, moschatel, wood-sage, wood-sorrel, wood-saxifrage, and also of countless un-recognizable sap-filled vegetable stalks. The air was alive with the muffled murmur, now loud, now soft, of the race of flies, each separate insect of the petty multitude steering this way and that, on untraceable quests of love or hunger. Dittany lay now indolently reclining under the rustling branches with her laces still loosened, her sweet body, after such impassioned usage, languid, fragrant, and relaxed. My senses ached to see her there so idly defenceless, rumpled, sense-drugged, looking dreamily up at the leaf-fretted summer sky, her head resting on one of her hands.

We had had one hour to spend and it was over, swift-passing as an April shower, as always when Dittany and I were together alone.

Say, is there aught that can convey
An image of its transient stay?

.   .   .

79

'Tis a shuttle in its speed ;
'Tis an eagle in its way,
Darting down upon its prey.

Whenever we were alone, hours became minutes, and minutes seconds. I had to teach myself to remember this on those occasions when a preliminary silence, charged with significance, would suddenly fall between us. It would then be no longer wise for me to rely upon clocks or watches for measuring time. From the moment that I kissed her first, from the moment that the scent of her body came to me as it were like rose-flushed white-clover found in a hayfield when the men and jangling horses have all left, I would be lost to the common world. After the very first touch had passed between us I would have no further power of calculation. My moments with Dittany seemed to share in eternity, and yet more richly still did they belong to the fugitive now of the life of this corn-planted planet. I kissed her that morning till she was tired out. I kissed her ' by the pot ' as the old expression has it, that is, holding her head between my hands by her two ears, by those two ears that she always kept so closely hidden under her hair and which were, for all that I ever knew, ' loave ' or ' prick ' in shape ; and then sometimes I would kiss her anywhere, everywhere, as best I might, so full I was of joy.

The sunlight fell upon her face, and the shadow of a tall pink-campion waved and flickered across her Orion-sealed forehead fairer than that 'full star that ushers in the even.' One hand was shading her eyes. As I looked at her I could see that her softly curving chin was covered with almost invisible hair like the down on one of the odorous peaches that my father would bring in to my mother fresh gathered from the kitchen-garden wall. And below the beautiful curve of her small chin was a sheltered area that continually held my vision, so inviolable did this part of her neck appear, less blemished than the lip argent of a Madonna lily across which an enamel-sharded garden-beetle might tread with pricking feet. My very bones were idolatrous of this morsel of mortal matter more admirable than the under side of a snow-finch's wing. Suddenly her whole attention was awakened as though she had seen an angel in the sky. 'It's a bird,' she cried excitedly, 'a white bird.' I looked up between the tree-tops expecting to see a dove from Norton Mill, but, instead, a large gull passed across the open space flying towards the sea. It was a rare thing in those days for one of these birds to traverse the Montacute district. Only once had I known such a thing to happen, and then we had all come running to the house calling our father from his study and our mother from her sewing to watch the hungry ocean fowl breast its way southward and seaward far up over the inland flower-beds, where humming-bird hawk moths flickered and poised over sultry geraniums. 'I think that must be a bad omen,' she said gravely, when the bird had finally disappeared in the direction of the Chinnocks. I reminded her that the unlucky bird John Oxenham had seen had been a white dove. 'The sight of a white sea-gull,' I said, 'ought to be read as a sign of good fortune.' 'How can you tell? I don't know,' she replied, rising impetuously from the ground. A moment later, however, she had thrown her arms about my neck—'Anyhow, I don't care,' she said.

> *O lovely and immaculate lady,*
> *I have no answer to give to you,*
> *Save the trampled grass and the boughs shady ;*
> *And nothing I used to know is true.*

The ambiguous lines of poetry recklessly spoken, the free spontaneous gesture and the fragrance of her neck, like lilac in the sun, revived my body's memory of its recent meeds. She became aware of its renewed eagerness. 'No, no, we mustn't, we mustn't,' she whispered nervously, 'we must go now or we shall be late. Besides, I want to visit the changeling pool we came to see,' she said, with a smile that was tender and yet at the same time not without regret. 'We will have to come

another day for that,' I answered. 'It is difficult to
find, and very overgrown on all sides.'—'I know I shall
now never see it,' she responded ruefully. Her voice
still had a hint of reproach in it. I tried to reassure
her. 'We will come especially to see the pool and
nothing else,' I explained. 'I know we shall never
reach it,' she continued. 'We never could, not on
Monday, Tuesday, Wednesday, Thursday, Friday, Saturday, or Sunday, take more than a few steps in such a
lovely dragon-fly wood without making love, and so we
will never get there.' She stood before me with eyes so
full of an authentic sadness that I was more than ever
bewildered. Seeing this she became at once gentle, kissing
my frowning forehead. With her head shadowed by the
constellated leaves, and with her feet upon the woodland
mould, she seemed to embody all the undefined delights
that my spirit had ever craved, and I became overwhelmed
by a sensation of ineffable happiness. It was no celestial
happiness that surrounded us. It was an earth happiness,
golden, all-embracing—a benison from gods older and
wiser than Jesus. Her level eyes seemed lightly to carry
the burden of everything lovely and free—snowdrops
in the rain, seaweed, ground-ivy in a February ditch,
blackberries in a basket, river-rushes ! Surely all the
sweets of June were encompassed within the fresh-
laundered whiteness of her dress.

As we clambered together down the steep side of the wood, what did we care for omens ? Our youth was so sanguine that it could not be intimidated by rumours of disaster. Such misgivings served but to add to our passion. The intensity of the love that we felt for each other cancelled all apprehensions except the apprehension of wasting a single opportunity of indulging it to the last quivering fulfilment. We reached the lane and had only a few yards to walk before we arrived at Tinker's Bubble. It was here that the overflow from the fairy pool burst out of the wood, its stream being carried over the wall of the sandy lane in the hollowed-out trunk of a young larch tree. Emily used to take us here on our nursery walks, pushing us when we were tired in a three-wheeled open perambulator large enough to carry three of us side by side. I remember once we came at Easter-time and picked ' pussy willows,' or ' palms,' as she taught us to call them, and brought them back with a bunch of daffodils from the Battlefield, to be placed in a large china bowl on the nursery table.

It was past twelve o'clock and yet the water that fell from the rude wooden spout in one continuous flow was ice-cold. The dust of the lane was darkened with its splashings. I made a cup of my hand as I had often seen my father do for my mother on his summer holiday walks, and she drank, this creature of an hour, more rare than

84

ever was the nymph Eurydice before her fateful race,—
fly, little maiden ! fly away across the snake-grass fells
of ancient Greece. When Dittany's thirst was satisfied,
when, with a last swift rippling sip she had raised her head,
laughing to feel the water run down her chin, I let the
gushing fountain splash over my own scalp. The water
was chill. It wetted my flannel shirt. This fountain-
stream seemed to celebrate our happy solacings in the
wood, its bright sparkling waters giving, so it appeared
to my romantic fancy, a sort of wild consecration to the
love that we felt for each other.

I I

*For oure tyme is a very shadow that passeth awaye,
and after our ende there is no returnynge, for it is fast
sealed, so that no man commeth agayne. Come on
therefore, let us enjoye the pleasures that there are, and
let us soone use the creature like as in youth . . . Let
us leave some token of oure pleasure in every place,
for that is oure porcion, els gett we nothinge.*

THE BOKE OF WYSDOME

THE MEMORIES OF THAT FAR-AWAY SUMMER MORNING in Norton Covert had occupied my waking thoughts during most of the night. I had not coughed much, but I had slept only fitfully. A nurse had arrived the day before from Weymouth and through the hours of darkness she sat on a chair at the end of the shelter wrapped about with rugs. If for a moment my mind left its reviewings I would find myself looking at the muffled-up figure of this strange young woman sitting silent against the stars of the August night. I would raise my hand for my glass spitting-bowl and in a moment she would be holding it to my mouth, or my parched throat would become intolerably dry and I would whisper for a drink and she would carry to my lips a tea-cup full of fresh milk, and at the taste of it immediately I would escape from those bedridden hours, and be lying again in the Terrace-Walk of Montacute Vicarage with the elder-blossoms holding up their pallid faces, round as moons, flat against the orchard hedge. Then a period would pass, and when again I would open my eyes it would be to see the whiteness that was heralding another day. I would then be aware that a solemn stillness had fallen upon the ancient hills, and soon, as it had been since the earliest epochs of the world's creation, the presence of the dawn would slowly be felt, and, moment by moment, on the high upland opposite, the forms of the cattle would become more clearly outlined. In the religious gravity of that half light I would lean back upon my pillows, untroubled, tranquil, as if in very truth I realized that I was part and parcel of that vast procession that included in its wide compass all tremulous life. Suddenly, however, my serenity would be disturbed by a fresh impediment in my breathing and I would know that my chest was once more filling up with blood and, until I had gathered a moiety of fortitude, I would be possessed by what Bunyan calls ' mind-horror ' to feel the vital animation that I loved so passionately flow so fast from my body.

The nurse, alarmed by the reiteration of my choking coughs, would pull the string that went through a window into the cottage and was attached to the handle of the old dinner-bell that had once belonged to my grandfather's house at Northwold, and my sister would come to me with a sponge-bag filled with ice that had been procured from a Weymouth fish-shop, and as I felt my ribs freeze with the impact of it the violence of the attack would gradually subside and I would be able to lie back and wait for Alyse, who would always be at my bedside before the sun rose.

Peace and again peace, and it would seem to my tried spirit security enough not to be struggling for my life *at that very moment*, and I would look at the misty distant hills on the northern horizon and at the garden webbed with gossamer as it always was after the torrid sunshine of the previous day, ' the day in its hotness ' continuing so regularly all through that summer, and giving the impression, the alternation of night with day and day with night, of the earth's deep breathing, of the rhythmical inhaling and exhaling, exhaling and inhaling of the great globe itself.

★　　★　　★

Fragments of days I would remember, occasions when Dittany and I had been together but had had no opportunity for any love-making. Sometimes she came to tea with us, sometimes at her home we would meet, for I used to be asked to their tennis parties. Strange old Somersetshire women would be watching the progress of the games, rows upon rows of them, rustling in gowns of expensive silks and smelling of Victorian vinaigrettes mitigated by a faint aroma of the proud sun-warmed leather which their clothes retained from the upholstery of the wide-open carriages, of the carriages, which, after a while, would begin bearing them away again to their various houses, smoothly and comfortably conveying them between the soft hedgerows of the roads and lanes of the old historic county.

I did not dislike the company of these incredibly old women. Bless the King and all his men! I knew very well and accepted as inevitable their narrow, self-interested, anti-social minds, I knew how worldly they were, and how if they could, they would desperately oppose everything that belonged to what was gracious in life, everything that was remote from the surface of their own artificial formalities. He that would have eggs must endure the cackling of hens. Most of all it diverted them to hear of any scandalous love-affairs ; tales of this kind they would greet with the shrill laughter of a crew of broomstick, black-cat witches. Their vitality was astonishing, the vitality of these old, old women who ought to have been on their knees praying to God, but who preferred to chatter together, like corbies on a gable. They were pretentious, ignorant, ostentatious; contemptuous of their inferiors, full of blandishments for anybody of superior rank or superior social eminence, a feminine folk with an inherited instinct for social deportment, but utterly entoiled by the more primitive and least desirable human emotions; unstable of mind, obstinate of nature, as eager to show themselves off as children, their interest concentrating for the most part upon their own rattling conversation, and the momentary effect it might have upon their neighbours. Yet for all their silken petticoats and elaborate headdresses they would look homely enough; a row of homely old women who were not ashamed to scratch their ankles when the midges began to snap, half an hour or so before the appearance of their broughams round the corner from the stable.

I couldn't take my eyes off Dittany, but I would try to avoid being caught watching her. I would help to hand about the bread-and-butter, and cake, and clotted-cream sandwiches. When we were separated we would both talk as foolishly as the rest, but if ever we were near each other we would be silent, she darting at me strange swift glances from some land 'where wind never blew, nor cocks ever crew.' How could we bear so much as to hear each other's voices in such surroundings?

I have seen the young at play in their secret garden,
Where the tall white unicorns come, and the phœnix flies.
I have seen the scarlet mouth that was curled for singing,
And the proud bright head, and the careless beautiful eyes.

Once I remember how a ball was lost from the lower
court. It had been hit over the wire-netting by a soldier
who wore a large gold signet-ring on one of his muscular
fingers and whose forearm was thickly grown over with
black hairs. The ball had gone bounding away into the
shrubbery. Much luck can come in a short time, and
we not thinking on it. Dittany rose from her seat to
go to look for the ball and I followed as unobtrusively
as I could. As soon as I was near her, 'delicious, wanton,
amiable, fair,' she began to laugh. 'Come,' she said, 'we
just have time,' and, abandoning all thought of the lost
ball, she led me through the laurels, staining her white
sleeves with the green of their damp round branches,
until we came out by a rubbish heap where the mown
grass from the lawns was emptied. She laid a plank over
the heap, so that she would not sink into the steaming
midden, and climbed on to the high wall behind. I
followed in astonishment, all alert to divine her plan.
The wall overlooked a meadow put up for hay, a large,
free, opulent meadow prostrate and bland in the afternoon's prodigal sunshine. She ran along the wall till

she reached the roof of a barn that stood in the field below. By the side of this barn was an ancient oak, still alive, though its top had long ago been blown away. The rim of the decapitated trunk was about ten feet from the coping of the wall. Without telling me what she was going to do, Dittany, holding to a branch, swung herself across the yawning gap and, clinging fast to certain other small branches, climbed lightly on to the oak and disappeared from sight into the tree's interior. I was amazed, for I had not even known the oak to be hollow, and, copying her movements, presently I found myself standing at her side within a circular chamber of a perfect wooden tower. As I remember the tree was hollow to a depth of about ten feet from its top.

I could not speak. I could do now what I had been longing to do all the afternoon. I suffered, I knew well, from a thirst I could never hope to quench, the smell of her hot body after her tennis playing strengthened my body into a passionate ardour. Over and over again I kissed her. She kept asking me where I had thought she was leading me. This evidently was her present paramount preoccupation, to measure exactly the amount of surprise I had experienced in my recent scramble at her flying heels. Her mocking laughter was ravishing to me, her cheeks so flushed, and her naked arms so white. Tarry a little that we may make an end the sooner. All was silent in the tree as we clung to each other in a transport of shameless indulgence, so real, so real :

> *He to whom your soft lip yields,*
> *And perceives your breath in kissing,*
> *All the odours of the fields*
> *Never, never shall be missing.*

★   ★   ★

Lying there in my shelter on the downs with the hours of the hot August passing, I tried to recapture every sensation I had then felt. Always over all was the strength of the love I had for her, a love so uncompromising that nothing that belonged to her or had been even remotely connected with her could ever have repelled me. No thought conjured to mind by the neurotic malice of Jonathan Swift could have seemed to me repulsive when I had to do with her body. Christian theologians assert that they experience strange mystical ecstasies as they contemplate the being of Jesus ; I underwent just such enthusiasms in the living presence of this girl. How I could have hovered over her bed, watching for her eyelids to open, how I could have washed her body wherein all was purity, below as well as above her waist, ' she is so bricht of hyd and hue.' Before I had my hæmorrhage, all through the summer, I had felt irresistible impulses to pray, impulses that were imperative and not to be with-stood, impulses that would draw me out on to the downs at all hours. These quaint oracular compulsions were nothing to what I used to experience in the presence of Dittany.

> *Let fools thy mystic form adore,*
> *I know thee in thy mortal state.*

The simple thought of her made me mad. She was no abstract conception, she was a creature I *could* worship, a creature of positive perishable flesh that I could apprehend with all my senses :

> *Her cheekes lyke apples which the sun hath rudded,*
> *Her lips lyke cherryes charming men to byte,*
> *Her brest like to a bowle of creame uncrudded*
> *Her paps lyke lyllies budded.*

It was as natural to my living body to adore her living body as it was to eat bread. The sight of any part of her could excite me, her long eyelashes, so blue, all through the sunshine-day lifting so lightly up and down, up and down, over her soft violet eyes—the light down on her arms inherited from an animal ancestry, as a protection against rain !

She made me promise to stay in the hollow tree for ten minutes after she had left so that we might reappear from

94

different directions and at different times. I could hear scarcely anything of the garden-party from where I was ; the birds everywhere were beginning their evening songs and like ' a haunted bell ' a cuckoo was calling. There was also the sound of a distant trotting along the road. My spirit trembled, the broad band of sunlight that fell across the inner side of my prison appeared so treacherous and transitory. My exultant happiness was constantly being tempered by the trembling thought of possible separation. It was as though I were in a dancing meadow with thunder all the time working up behind the tall shrouded elms ! Unless I could be with Dittany every minute of the day and night I knew I must be tormented. Only when I was with her, when I knew I had but to put out my hand to touch her, could I hope for peace of body and mind. We were two shadows that had met in a tough world of wood and stone and must contrive for our felicity. As to marriage, how could any one agree to my marrying her unless we in desperation ran away together ? And if we ran away, how could we live, how could I feed her when I had no money, and no profession ? Lips, however red, must be fed. It was not to be considered. We must be happy in the present. And yet if our destiny went as we wished, if Fate allowed me to tend her, to care for her always, how long would the always be ? How many generations of men had been swallowed up since the original sprout of this great oak tree split its acorn ? When it was a sapling in this same field, the very dialect of the country had been different and the roads were being traversed by knights in armour, and jongleurs, and Saxon peasants with cross-strapped hosen. If we both were lucky enough to live till eighty we should have had no time at all.

12

Sweet lover mine, I cannot make believe.
With all my heart I love you, nor deceive
And you may kiss me over when you please,
Within your arms fain would I find mine ease.

Whispering wind and branches meet,
Whoso love limb to limb sleep sweet.

EARLY MEDIÆVAL FRENCH LYRIC
Translated by CLAUDE COLLEER ABBOTT

I REMEMBER CLEARLY AN OCCASION IN EARLY JUNE WHEN
Dittany came to tea with us. I had persuaded my
sister to ask her. My father always preferred to have
his meals indoors, but that afternoon he had arranged to
walk to Chilthorne Domer and so we were free to take
tea on the tennis-lawn, my mother, and my sister Gertrude,
Dittany and myself.

I have in my cottage four cups and saucers of the old
Montacute tea-set and I think it was the appearance during
my illness of one of these fragile cups with its familiar
red rim that made me recall so vividly this particular
afternoon.

My mother was in a happy mood. From the first she

had liked Dittany ; her gentleness appealed to her, and the romantic look of the girl with her absent-minded ways, her misty eyes, and the unexpected beauty that in moments of animation would suddenly light up her face. I sat on a garden-seat sheltered by a bush ; my mother, my sister, and Dittany sat on garden chairs.

> Be she sitting, I desire her
> For her state's sake ; and admire her
> For her wit if she be talking.

Mary Hockey had set the tea and soon appeared coming down the steps under the clematis-covered arch with sponge-buns hot from Ellen's oven. I liked to see her good-natured face under her servant's cap which nestled upon her head a little awry. From my position I could watch the great cloud procession drifting across the heavens, far up above the sycamore ; enormous white mountains, snowy mountains with wide-shadowed sea-valleys lying between them, and chalk-white promontories projecting into summer bays motionless as glass. The sun was still high and the shadow of the monkey-puzzle lay sprawling like a crooked octopus upon the warm, velvet-smooth grass of the lawn.

The sound of my mother's voice, of my sister's voice, and of Dittany's voice came to me soft and soothing as the murmur of dozing doves. In the mud steps that led up the grassy bank under the monkey-puzzle I had often as a child prodded out yellow clay. We used to model figures out of this clay and persuade Ellen to bake them for us. And now under the grey eider-duck abdomens of those white floating clouds I was realizing the present, looking at Dittany happy and radiant, chattering and sipping her tea, entranced by the frock she had on, and with a thrilling awareness of the girlish body it covered. Often on such occasions I would be afraid that I would not be allowed to live long enough to be alone with her again. Our joy was of the kind that the jealous gods never gladly suffer.

When tea was over we walked round the garden together. We went through the pear garden. The little shed we used to call the Mabelulu, where I had played with May and Bertie, was standing under the kitchen-garden wall deserted. The Jerusalem artichokes were already tall. I explained to her how as children we would come here every day of the holidays, and how my brother Bertie had designed and built the little house with its cellar and bay-window. And I told her how once in the winter when we two boys were clearing the Mabelulu garden of rubbish I threw a living lobworm into the bonfire and how my brother had observed me doing this, and how he had scolded me—a serious-eyed little boy with a red scarf about his neck and dressed in an old garden suit,

99

delivering a true word to another little boy attentively listening beneath a leafless fruit-tree, in a pair of patched mother-made knickerbockers damp at the knees from continual heedless contacts with the wintry soil.

> *Even bolder yet am I :*
> *Her white hand I took her by ;*
> *A leafy orchard led her soft within*
> *And then I kissed her mouth and kissed her chin.*
> *' Lady, I love you more than any can ;*
> *Ah, if not me, then love no other man.'*

We walked through the top orchard and from there into the field behind the kitchen-garden wall. We stood together for a little under the walnut-tree. I showed her each of the great branches which bore nursery names—the dining-room, the boudoir, the hall ! It was my sister Nelly who had so christened them ; it was also she who had dragged, pulled, and coaxed me, even as an infant, into ' her attic,' so that strangers coming up the station road had stopped at the Vicarage to ask if my mother knew that one of her babies was at play in the topmost twigs of the high-towering tree. Dittany was always full of attention when I spoke of my childhood, perhaps because she had so lately been a child herself. How cool it was to stand beneath the shadowed cirque of the giant walnut, cool as a cellar with its round carpet of coarser grass. When we looked up all was green, green and again green, shielded from the sun's rays by a wealth of gypsy staining leaves, salubrious and aromatic when crushed in the hand.

Dittany leaned her back against the tree's smooth bark and stretched out her arms.

> *A branch of sovereign dittany she bore*
> *From Ida gathered on the Cretan shore.*

She looked at me with eyes laughing and confident. Had Marsyas, I wonder, a *hornless* sister, white as a peeled willow, who, stepping rashly from the Phrygian brake, had dared with plaintive pipings to put to the hazard her own silver skin ; until by the evening, with storm clouds driving over tree-top leaves, the forests echoed to the shrill lamentations of satyr and hamadryad who, trembling, watched the casual departure of the twice victorious god with a pelt so dear and bright cast careless across an easy elbow ?

That afternoon Dittany was lovely, was like starlight upon water, moonshine upon dew, sunlight upon glittering mountain snow. How could I help but praise her to her face there where she stood ? I had not seen anything more unwonted, more startling in its glancing grace, since Bertie and Willie and I in this very glebe had watched a golden oriole settle upon a branch of the old Tauntonblack apple-tree near the summer-house—a sight most wonderful, not only because of its rareness, scarce to be seen again in the space of a hundred years, but also for the vision of such a Hesperidean a missel-thrush come to rest in the foliage of so homely a tree. To the imaginations of us sauntering Sunday-afternoon bird-nesters, this was as quickening a vision as Blake's of the prophet Ezekiel suddenly and gloriously present in his dooryard lilac.

I said I would show her the stables and the loft of the stables. I knew why, and so did she. We went through the saddle-room. The loft was large and ran along the whole length of the building. At the farther end were piled old family travelling trunks. One was a black, long-shaped box about the size of a dwarf's coffin which had been used by my grandfather in the coaching days. As a child I had often opened its lid and sat in it, pretending that it was a boat. The loft could be made quite light by throwing open the door of the large square window, designed for receiving fodder for the Goodden carriage-horses ; but I had no wish to open this door now. We clambered to the top of the great pile of hay and there in a nest we lay.

I could never prolong the preliminary minutes of our being alone together, resolve to do so as much as I might. I would forget everything as I ran heedless along those

paths of breathless delight, impatient as a boy after
butterflies.

Sometimes I sing, sometimes I stay
To watch the flickering butterflies ;
Glamour has lit the world to-day,
The golden sun is in my eyes.

How I loved to feel her burning cheeks as I kissed them,
how I loved to hold her in my arms, to touch with
trembling hands her soft, unkissed body so lightly covered.
Always I was bewildered with an indescribable sense of
exultant life.

' Her waist is a most tiny hinge of flesh, a winsome
thing and strange ; apt in my hand warmly to lie
it is a throbbing neck whereby to grasp the belly's
ample vase (that urgent urn which doth amass for
whoso drinks, a dizzier wine than should the
grapes of heaven combine with earth's madness)—
'tis a gate unto a palace intricate (whereof the
luscious pillars rise which are her large and shapely
thighs) in whose dome the trembling bliss of a
kingdom wholly is.'

At last we were content to be still in a happy state of utter
forgetfulness, of forgetfulness of everything except that
we were together. The hay upon which we were lying

smelt sweet. I could hear the starlings on the roof above us. I knew the hole in which they had a nest every year. It was below the eaves of the stable at the top corner of the wall above the greengage tree. Through the cracks and crevices of the old tiles the sunlight of the summer's evening splintered itself into the half darkness in slanting line-levels of gilded motes. We remained for a long time there together, our heads close in happy trance. Reluctantly, at last, I climbed off our bed to look at my watch by one of the shafts of light. She thought she still had an hour. Wishing to steal its fulness from every moment that we had I suggested that we should walk again in the orchard. She made me turn towards the door while she arranged her dress. In this strictness of hers I always found delight. Even with my head scrupulously averted, how conscious I was of her doings. When at last she said she was ready I scrambled back to her and kissed her again and again.

We went through the orchards, the cows had returned after milking. They moved slowly about under the low branched trees, their tails switching ; beasts of piety abroad in a world of fragrant herbage. Next to love, quietness. The evening air was sweeter to breathe than a bean field's breath. Nobody now would think to look for mistletoe, so thick clustered were the myriad round coarse apple leaves. We climbed down the wall into

Cole's orchard and I showed her the slope where as a little boy I had once played by myself with the large family toboggan. There were rabbits everywhere. The orchards lay in the pride of their summer luxury, they were as soothing to the mind as the distant sound of a flute. We passed the old ruined house and stood under the tall beech trees. The sun was drawing towards the ridge of Ham Hill and its radiance was slanting in yellow arrowy lines between the grey trunks. The presence of that still momentary light from the sinking sun made me sad, and to forget my uncertainty I put my arm about Dittany and kissed her.

I had not noticed that my father on his way back from Chilthorne was coming up through the orchard behind me. When I did hear his steps and looked round I saw that he had deliberately turned away from us towards the old house. He greeted us both with benevolence. I was embarrassed but he was so charming to Dittany that, as we walked by his side, I soon felt reassured. He gave her some sprays of the hedgerow honeysuckle that he had picked. 'It really is a most beautiful evening, Llewelyn, see how the sun shines upon the branches of the old acacia-tree. The country is looking very well. I found good Mr. Palmer at home and he hopes to see you soon. There is a young man who has come to his neighbourhood whom he would like us to see something of, and I thought, all being well, you and I might call upon him next Saturday afternoon.'

We soon reached the little wicket-gate that led to the Vicarage drive. Dittany now said good-bye to my father, but I was disinclined to part and offered to walk some of the way back with her to her home, leaving my father, with his wild flowers in his hand, to be welcomed by my mother at the front door while we two went out of the drive gate, letting it swing to, with its familiar click, clang, click.

I3

The flat transgression of a schoolboy, who being overjoyed with finding a bird's nest, shows it his companion and he steals it.

WILLIAM SHAKESPEARE

ON SATURDAY MY FATHER AND I DULY SET OUT UPON our expedition. We went down Hodder's lane, cool and shaded under its heavy foliage. Merely to think of the lane is to bring back to my mind memories. As a child with Emily I had clambered up and run along every one of its high roadside banks. Often in our schoolroom walks we had come this way ; my sister Marian and I, following in the wake of Miss Beales, pretending to be Sir Luda, Frank, and Amyas Leigh, characters from our favourite books. At the top of the lane there stood a large beech tree. It guarded a strip of woodland. We children often used to wonder what we might find at the end of this wood and once in the Easter holidays my brother Bertie and I had explored it.

We had told each other that we would find a heap of armour at its end, but what we did find were cowslips. We had never seen cowslips growing in a wood before.

They lacked the native purity of those that come up in dairy fields. They were much taller and more luscious, with thick juicy stalks. We were astonished to see them. We had come pushing our way through the brambles and suddenly there we were in an open place quietly blessed with the beauty of these flowers. The unexpected sight made a deep impression upon both of us. All through my life it became a kind of symbolic promise of what might happen, of the secret and unbelievable rewards that life could offer to me if I were willing to adventure. It was perhaps for this reason that those congregated cow-slips interspersed with Granfer Griggles, as Dorset children call wood orchises, came to be connected in my mind with Dittany. From under the great tree it was possible, looking southward across the mill-stream valley, to view Montacute Vicarage with the drive just showing above the kitchen-garden wall. Indeed, it was from this position that, as a little boy, I had seen the carriage at the front door which had brought my brother John from Sherborne School, sick even in those early times, with a disordered digestion.

Before making his call my father proposed to collect a subscription for his Church Missionary Society from an elderly gentleman whose talents were principally exercised in business transactions, but who, in Victorian fashion, kept also a wary eye on his prospects for a safe arrival in heaven, a prudence which prompted him to attend the village church twice every Sunday, and once a year to give a substantial subscription to my father's Society with the deferential self-interested intention of an African native chief presenting the local witch-doctor with propitiatory gifts. My father was relieved to get away from the old man's house. As soon as he was on the free side of the garden gate he walked off with long strides down the road, saying that he ' always found the worthy man very civil.' I recollect he came to a halt before a patch of rough ground by the side of the way to show me some camomile that was already in flower, as though he derived from the contemplation of the raggle-taggle yellow plant some sort of liberation of spirit. My thoughts, however, were immediately away to Dittany. They could not be kept from her, no, not for half an hour, and the little dusty flower put me in mind of the old song :

> *Your gown sall be the sweet-william,*
> *Your coat the camovine,*
> *Your apron a' the salluds neat*
> *That taste baith sweet and fine.*

Camovine I had been taught was the old word for camomile.

The name of the young man who had bought The

Grange was Randal Pixley. We entered the courtyard and rang the bell. A manservant led us into a large and pleasant room with doors opening out upon a walled-in garden. My father sat down upon a Queen Anne chair and gave me a look full of conspiring friendliness, as though to say, ' It will not be very long, Llewelyn, my boy, before we are out in the fields again.' I felt great affection for him as he sat there, his personality obstinately resistant to this new environment and his head looking so familiar. How often at Commemoration Days at Sherborne School I had seen him suddenly appear amongst a crowd of parents, seen him with a shock of recognition, my own father, with the side-whiskers of an older period on his grave, ancestral countenance, so unlike any corpulent business-man, or glib, well-groomed lawyer. My father's large country boots, made to measure by Mr. Boole the village cobbler, were now covered with white dust from the roadsides we had walked along, and very friendly they looked to me resting on the Turkish carpet. Through the doors at the end of a long stone-paved garden-path I presently caught sight of a young man approaching. My first impression of Randal Pixley was a favourable one. He was dressed in flannels and came sauntering up through the garden in an abstracted way. An elderly lady now appeared and by the time we had shaken hands with her the young man was also in the room. I noticed that his tie, a red one, had run in the wash. His aunt, Lady Lulworth, I did not care for so much. She was one of those women who talk without thinking, who will ask you questions and not take the trouble to listen to your answer. She kept up a continual flow of conversation, while, with dexterity, she went through certain necessary manipulations with the receptacle that held the flame under the kettle. I could see that my father did not care for her. He would answer her questions with slow gravity as though he intended to confound her by the sheer weight of his reserves. ' I have recently been visiting some relations of yours in Northamptonshire,' I heard her say. She referred to the Lilford Powyses ; and my father's odd pride prevented him from joining in her talk about them. Instead, he told us solemnly that his father had always attributed a weakness in his eyesight to his having ridden from Achurch to Cambridge in the face of an east wind. Lady Lulworth's tone under the disarming unworldliness and sober reserves of my father's way of talk soon lost something of its affable rattle.

Meanwhile I was observing the young man closely. He was not so old as I, but was already down from Oxford. I took to him at once. He was very intelligent, had brown hair and exceedingly vulnerable brown eyes. I can't tell what it was about him that won me from the first. Perhaps my sense that it was impossible to believe he could ever molest anyone by word or deed. He seemed to touch reality in a nonchalant manner and only at intervals, soon retiring to the removed personal dimension of his soul's natural dwelling. His head was very round, rounder than I remember having known a human head to be. He suggested that we two should take a turn in the garden. He liked me, I think, as much as I liked him. I remember he showed me a plant of rue, I had never seen rue before, or at least, had never identified it.

And halesome herbis upon stalkis greene ;
Yet leaf nor flower find could I nane of rew.

I asked him as casually as I could whether he was acquainted with the plant called dittany. I thought he might possibly have seen it in St. John's Garden at Oxford, where, according to one herbalist book, it was said to be especially cultivated. He had never heard of it and indeed was entirely ignorant of the wealth of antique magical lore associated with it. For some time we continued standing side by side, silently contemplating the sultry flower-borders with every stalk, leaf, and petal, hot from the afternoon's sun. The garden was surely a lovely one, sheltered as it was on all sides by high walls.

Whenever the valerian is in flower on the wall which you pass as you come into Preston, near Weymouth, opposite the Ship Inn, I think of that enclosed Somersetshire parterre. Valerian grew on the top of the wall overlooking the lane in great abundance, and my father, as we were leaving, told me that at Stalbridge they used to call this flower 'Kiss me quick.' This unexpected confidence especially pleased the mood I was then in.

Randal Pixley directed me to a round fish-pond. There we sat on a white seat watching the carp navigating themselves indolently between the leaves of the water-lilies. Like sensible young men we talked about girls. His conversation was an odd mixture of reserve and licence. Whenever I am attracted to a person I always am inclined to be indiscreet. I seem to want to reward them for the sympathy they have aroused in me by showing my confidence in some exceptional way, by proving to them, as it were, how much I trust them.

While we were talking a little green frog put its head out of the water and began to pull itself up on to a flat water-lily leaf ; like a Lilliputian shipwrecked sailor it kept endeavouring with crooked elbows to get a purchase on the emerald island. We both watched with interest the resolution of this plump outlandish tread-water mariner.

Open the door, my hinny, my heart,
Open the door, my own darling,
Remember the words you spake to me
In the meadow by the well-spring.

For some reason its quaint fairy-story presence in the sunny pond reminded me of the happiness of my days with Dittany, and I suddenly felt a strong desire to confide my good fortune to this urbane young man whose tastes and opinions were evidently so much in harmony with my own. ' There is,' I said, ' one girl in the neighbourhood who has nothing whatever to do with this period. She is by far the most unreal girl that I've ever seen, a girl who cannot be related with the commonplace, a girl who goes dreaming along these Somerset lanes and through these Somerset woods like one enchanted. She reminds me of Nimue who so besotted Merlin. You remember, he would let the damsel of the lake have no rest. I quoted Malory's very words : 'And always Merlin lay about the lady to have her maiden-head.' It was enough.

What I said evidently caught the imagination of my companion. ' What is her name ? ' he bluntly asked. In a flash I was given a premonition of my folly. I hesitated for a moment and then told him.

14

Though but a shadow, but a sliding,
Let me know some little joy !
We that suffer long annoy
Are contented with a thought
Through an idle fancy wrought :
O let my joys have some abiding !

JOHN FLETCHER

ONE OF THE HAPPIEST DAYS THAT DITTANY AND I SPENT together was on the river Yeo. We had arranged to be with each other from dawn till evening. I told Ellen that I was going out for the whole day and asked her to make egg, honey, and lettuce sandwiches overnight and to put out supplies of sponge-cake, buns, and raisins, ready for me on the kitchen dresser. With the idea of sleeping out of doors I had ordered a garden tent. It had come that morning, but I had not had time as yet to put it up so was forced to go to bed as usual in the nursery. I might, however, have been sleeping in a hammock woven of flowering clematis cords, so strongly did the room carry the odour of those little white blossoms thick clustering about the window.

For a long time I could not get to sleep. A lover's soul
lives in the body of his mistress. I felt as I used to at
school on the last day of the term. I could not wait for
the hours to pass. I would put my head on the pillow,
first lying on my left cheek and then on my right, closing
my eyes ; but try as I might I could not sleep. Then I
would say to myself, ' Well, I don't care if I don't sleep
. . . I will stay awake all night,' and I would turn over,
and, lying on my back, listen to the dulcet silence of the
summer garden. The sash-window was up, and over the
muffling folds of the clematis I could see the spreading
branches of the acacia, against the dimness of the night.
There was a moon almost full, but many stars also were
illuminating the cold midnight lawns, the bark of the
trees alive with insects under dark rustling branches, and
the crinkled sapless moss on the old garden walls. How
actual it all was to me outside. I could almost feel the
air, the soft summer garden air, pass through the shining
leaves of the Portugal-laurel, could feel it turn up the
tiny hairs on the plump, hirsute bodies of moths scaveng-
ing with gleaming, goblin eyes through the crowded
spears of the lavender bush that porcupine-like bristled
at the centre of the Crescent-bed. How lovely, how
consecrated on a summer's night, are the interspaces
between dreaming garden trees ! As a child I had played
in this room. It was here I had looked at my first picture-

book, it was here that I had seen my nurse, as it were an angel in a vision, entering from the night-nursery in her Sunday apron. I knew every inch of it, the particular shapes of the marks and spots on the window-sill, where in the shivering precipitations of atomic matter the old Goodden varnish had been withdrawn ! I knew each irregularity of the darker tracings that showed in the marble of the fire-place tiles. I knew the picture of the farmyard cock and hen, the table of plain deal which we used to revolve upside down like a gigantic turtle, balancing it on a hard hassock and running round and round, clutching the one of its four legs which was thinner than the others. At any moment I could rise and sit upon the sofa of fairy-story-reading memories, a sofa covered over with webbed hair from the manes and tails of horses —shiny, slippery, and jet black. Those hairs had been pulled from mares and geldings who had plunged and snorted and stood about by the hedges of green paddocks long before I had been born. In this room I had carried my brother Willie on my shoulders and let him fall, and had witnessed my mother's alarm as, at the sound of his cries, she came running to the room to see a green bump rise up on his forehead as large as a heron's egg. In this room I had, with cradle straw scarce out of my breech, outwitted my brother Bertie over a matter of three biscuits. We—Bertie, May, and myself—had been play-

117

ing with building bricks when Emily came with three sugar biscuits which were to be given to us when we had tidied up the room. She placed the biscuits on the chest-of-drawers, and presently I noticed that the largest had been slipped under a book out of sight by my brother. Waiting my chance, baby though I was, I stretched up and put into my brother's chosen hiding-place the smallest of the biscuits, being myself alert silently to consume the largest before the last of the bricks had been put away. It was an incident my brother never forgot all through his life, so deeply impressed was he that so newly-born an infant could contrive to be master of such a knavery.

Many a merry meeting
My love and I have had;
She was my only sweeting,
She made my heart full glad.

I was wide awake at five o'clock. To my surprise I found that I had slept soundly for several hours. I got up at once. Dittany had promised to try to meet me by Bob Chaffey's white gates in Marsh Lane at half-past six. I walked to Marsh Lane through the meadows by the station-stream. It was a perfect midsummer morning. The sun was already 'kissing with golden face the meadows green.' When I looked back over the station-field I could see the track of my footsteps in the dew.

The turned-up ends of my flannel trousers were soaked and covered with grass-seeds. Over the pollarded willows, over the hedges, over the dairy meadows, and over the hay-fields that had been already mown came the singing of birds. My ears might have been licked by grass-snakes and slow-worms, so sensitive had they become. The joy of the birds was without stint. They sang like creatures enchanted, like creatures thrilling with ecstasy from claw to feather-tip. It seemed as though the early sunshine had utterly redeemed those Somersetshire meadows. They were light as paddocks of Arcady. They quivered, danced, and laughed, and at the same time they retained their solid actuality, thick bespattered with cow-pats loose and emerald green. I have never forgotten the lesson I learned that morning. Of course men and women are created to be happy, their capacity for happiness is without bounds. The greatest villainies can be laid at the door of old men moralities, exaggerated beyond all reason by the clergy, and by mind-cramped masquerading judges with their ears hung about with white ewes' wool, all of them looking out at the world, as Rabelais says, through one hole. He preaches well who lives well, that is all the Divinity I know.

I passed the place where a tributary stream from the Tintinhull side of the railway-line comes through a culvert. As a little boy I had crawled with Bertie along the diminutive tunnel, holding in my hand a bucket full of sticklebacks for our aquarium. I knew well the intimate life of the little stream, its deep holes and shallow holes. I knew where the loaches were to be caught under the islands of rushes. I knew how the sticklebacks looked when you held them flickering in your hand, these marvellous little fish in miniature, with eyes, scales, fins in perfect proportion, such trout as a buttercup-high fairy might fish for, with a creel of woven quaking-grass hung about his shoulder.

I reached the lane. I had as yet seen no sign of human life, but now as I climbed the stile I could make out wisps of blue smoke curling up from Wulham's Mill. They are preparing their fires for heating their coppers, I thought, either for washing, or that they may have water ready for making sweet their dairy-pans and pails.

I soon reached our meeting-place, but nobody was there. I waited and waited, straining my eyes in trying to catch the first glimpse of her between the distant green hedges. She is not coming, I thought. She will never come. I waited as I had often waited in dreams with a half-conscious recognition at the back of my mind that the reality I was experiencing was of no very steadfast essence. I thought of the feathers of a dead hen-blackbird I had just seen by the side of the lane, caught on its nest, perhaps by a marauding stoat. These feathers would linger for a time, gnawed at by little hungry mice, examined and scattered by predatory crawling insects with minute retractile claws, and then as the winter advanced would be drenched, degraded, and disgraced still further.

> *All things making for Death's taking !*
> *—So the green-gowned faeries say*
> *Living over Blackmoor way.*

It was in this unreliable world of floating appearances, of shadowy apparitions, a world foredoomed to extinction, that I was now living.

> *She is walking in the meadow,*
> *And the woodland echo rings ;*
> *In a moment we shall meet.*

There she was ! No, it was someone from the farm, a dairy-maid in her milking-apron, but there she really and truly was a little way behind. I could see her unmistakably between the grass-green twigs of the hedge. It was teasing that this other should have appeared just at the same time. I had intended to run to meet Dittany and now I had first to pass this unknown young woman, had to pass her as though my business on that fine morning were in no way exceptional. Dittany must have felt much the same, for it was a very demure hand she put forward with an amused bow, stately and reserved, such as she used when we met at parties. I experienced the same shock of surprise that I always did at seeing her again. She was wearing her wide summer hat decorated with a blue ribbon, and a blue sash was about her thin cotton frock, a frock marked with little roses so small that they would have been suitable for that same stickle-back fisherman to have sent as a garden gift to his true love.

It was not long before the farm girl got over a field gate and we were alone. We then took each other's hand and went slowly down the lane. 'Think,' she said, 'what long hours we have before us. Do you know, when I saw you coming up the lane to meet me, a verse out of a love poem came into my head?' And as we walked with springing footsteps between the hedges she repeated the words :

I have loved the beauty of your talking,
All the words you said
Nested in my mind like blackbirds singing
Treasured in the head,
I remember all, I have remembered
Every word you said.

122

All your grace of mind and grace of body,
Patterns that your feet
Made on paths of fern on hills of bracken,
Counsels wise and sweet,
How your face looked brighter than the morning
I had come to meet.

As I listened to her voice it was as if I were holding happiness in my hands as a child holds up a sun-warmed apricot. Near the bridge where the railway crosses Marsh Lane, there is a gate hidden from view beneath a willow-tree. It was here that we kissed for the first time that day. The fields were golden with buttercups, and through the air, yellow and green under the sunshine, the birds went flying, now up, now down, with see-saw flights. I do not think the cuckoo was ever silent for more than five minutes.

Against the gate I held her, this lovely creature of my own kind. I was wildly, madly alive to the proximity of her body, of her body so close to mine, naked under her frock, her breasts as firm and explicitly rounded as wall fruit. Near is my kirtle but nearer is my smock. I knelt down. I threw my arms about her. She seemed to me transfigured. She was encompassed by my love. It was an aureole about her beautiful head, a girdle about her belly, and golden rings about her ankles. Her cheeks grew flushed, her eyes shone, she laughed to feel my love run over her as lightly and as gaily as moorland water in the sun.

15

For a girdle, tender leaves,
When the weather rained, grew green,
 Buttoned up with gold.
Cords of flowers swung above
Her wallet shapen all for love,
 And Love the giver bold.

EARLY MEDIÆVAL FRENCH LYRIC
Translated by CLAUDE COLLEER ABBOTT

W E HAD PLANNED TO WALK TO ILCHESTER. I
wanted to show her Roger Bacon's house.
We had our breakfast by the roadside at the
top of Hunger Hill. We sat in the ditch that shone with
dandelions. An old lilac-tree grew there, overhanging the
hedge at the end of the cottage garden. Between its
massed spiral flowers, so perfect in form and colour, we
could see the sky of infinity ! How it was that the
lilac was in flower I could not tell. The blossoms on
the lilac-bush by the tennis-lawn and the blossoms on
the bush near the juniper and the golden yew had long
since been scattered to nothing, each several rusty-
coloured corolla having slipped silently down to an
absolute disappearance in mould or grass. Was it perhaps

125

that the first burgeoning of the early buds of this particular
tree had been severely checked by the March winds blowing up from the Kingsmore dykes, where even the lank
legs of paddling herons could be numbed to their marrow
piths by the cold ? Or was the isolated, hill-top cottage
really inhabited by a fairy-tale witch, friendly to both of
us, a witch fairy who knew we would come at midsummer—a rook boy and goose girl—to sit munching and
talking under the tree's flowering branches ? This was
Dittany's idea as with dancing eyes fixed upon me she
recited the rhyming invocation :

> *Blow, breezes blow !*
> *Let Curdkin's hat go !*
> *Blow, breezes blow !*
> *Let him after it go !*
> *O'er hills, dales and rocks*
> *Away be it whirl'd*
> *Till my hazel locks*
> *Are all comb'd and curl'd.*

Across the valley Camelot was clearly visible, Camelot
and Corton Downs and Corton Beacon, and I saw in mind
the sheep grazing quietly on the sunny slopes of those far-
off hills in full prospect of the wide Wessex landscape,
sheep hot to the touch and with their woolly backs smelling of ancient securities ; sheep with mild herbivorous

mouths nuzzling after the sweetest grass on each high lawn freshened with thyme, and cooled by upland airs.

The Fosse Way always used to excite me. Straight as a pike-staff it descends into Ilchester. To strike the road with horseshoe or iron-shod boot is to hear the echoes of the marching legions. When years later I was approaching Rome and saw first the ruins of the ancient city the sense of direct contact with the Romans that I then felt was in no way more real than the impressions I had often received slap out of the past as I walked upon this west-country high-road dropping down to Ilchester. Where were now those old Romans so puissant and so practical ? They and their vaunted organization had vanished utterly like the blackbird's feathers in Marsh Lane. No wise man should ever be persuaded to expend his energy in further-ing the aggrandisement of his nation. The people who stress the importance of patriotism, of imperialism, are blind mouths. These values are not only meaningless but they are barbarous also, the values of the rat, of the wolf, the values of Satan. The simple, harmless, natural pleasures of life are alone of significance ; work, the gratification of our creature appetites, the propagation and upbringing of children, and what sensible hours we are able to spend, snatched from husbandry, sitting idle in the sun.

As we rested there laughing and talking like two
gypsies, laughing and eating lettuce and honey sand-
wiches and Ellen's little cakes, true obley cakes they were
to me, I thought how the very same feelings that were
now stirring my body must have been exactly repeated
every time that the Romans had halted here.

> Visioning on the vacant air
> Helmed legionaries, who proudly rear
> The Eagle, as they pace again
> The Roman Road.

The young centurions, impatient to reach their villas
where they knew southern ladies were loitering for them,
longing, loving ladies, with their dark eyes intent to
observe the flickering of a late afternoon lamp of clay, or
watching perhaps through the dim northern air one of the
newly imported pheasants strutting on rustling leaves at
the forest's edge. It is because the gift of life is too sweet
that we shuffle to make light of it. It is because the gift
of lust is too inebriate that the human race has been at such
pains to discredit it with precautionary mistrusts. Carnal
love between a man and woman is incomparably the
richest award, the highest experience that life has to offer
to any man. Always this simple truth has been acknow-
ledged by the wise, in cities, in forests, in hedge-ditches.
Here is no fairy gold to vanish at the touch. It is a

warrantable good. It is the same yesterday, to-day, and for ever, the one sufficient compensation for all the tears that have been shed upon the earth. Here is the ultimate satisfaction of man and beast, simple, understood by all.

One thing only spoilt the harmony of our walk down to Ilchester. I had been telling Dittany the hearsay about the spendthrift squire of Montacute, how he had gambled away the two farms we could see across the meadows on the right of us, by betting on a fly that was crawling up the window-pane in a Weymouth club on a rainy afternoon. The squire's fly, so the story ran, lost the race and friends who stood near heard the squire mutter the mysterious words, ' Good-bye, Sock and Beerly.' These were the names of the two farms which we could see over the water-meadows, and which, so it was said, had been sold to meet this debt of honour. I told her how the Phelipses used to own all the land about Montacute and a great deal of the land round Tintinhull. ' Tintinhull,' Dittany interjected ; ' it was somewhere near a village of that name that Mother said the young man came from, who called yesterday when I was out walking.'—' Do you remember the man's name ? ' I asked in as careless a voice as I could. ' Randal something,' she answered. ' Is the wind at that door ? ' I thought, ' Now, I begin to reap the reward of my folly ! ' Deeply did I curse my lack

129

of discretion. Of course my words had roused his interest, probably already this young man's head was dizzy with dreams about Dittany. Her casual remark troubled me. I kept saying to myself, ' But he has not even seen her yet.' Dittany felt that all was not right, and presently she put her hand on my wrist, saying ' What is it, Llewelyn ? I know that something is on your mind—you are thinking something.'—I lied, ' It is only because I know we will have to separate one day.'—' Never until I am dead.'— She spoke the words so seriously that I felt reassured at once and my good spirits came rushing back.

We now climbed on to the low wall that was on the right of the road. This wall was surmounted with flat flagstones and it was easy to walk along the top of it. We followed, one behind the other, Dittany before and I behind. Below us on the right was a deep dyke, a dyke typical of the methods used for draining this farthest arm of Sedgemoor. The reeds and rushes were so tall that they were often higher than the wall. Below the tall reeds were arrowhead plants, flowering rushes, pond weeds warm in the sun, with budding meadow-sweet and hemp agrimony congregated along the bank—all of them smelling of the green-mantled unseen water of the rhine which for weeks now had remained in a state of stagnant stillness, disturbed by nothing more violent than the somnambulent emergence of a crumple-faced dragon-fly, or the flicking of cheap tadpoles which, like diminutive whales, with small eyes and large mouths, passed blameless unrecorded hours in the darkened shallows.

It was now about ten o'clock. The sky was cloudless, and it was easy to see that by midday it would be very hot indeed. Dittany was carrying her hat in her hand, but I persuaded her to put it on her head. Already I could make out the eighteenth century farm-house which was rumoured to stand on the exact site of the old Bacon Manor House of mediæval times. Between the house and us the sun-motes danced their airy jigs above the dusty turnpike. In just such a way the atmosphere must have quivered before the eyes of other generations. In Ilchester churchyard lovers such as we lay dead skull by skull, each skull with empty eye-sockets large enough for the holding of the fattest Twelfth-night candles, skulls that once were fitted with eyeballs, those bright glassy instruments of the most startling of all the senses.

> *Wake, all the dead ! What ho ! what ho !*
> *How soundly they sleep whose pillows lie low !*
> *They mind not poor lovers, who walk above*
> *On the decks of the world in storms of love.*

How is it that those who are alive can never realize their chance beyond all chances, how is it that even the wisest of us are such fools that we take our own hour of exemption

131

from nothingness for granted : giving to the moments that race past at best but a listless attention! When we look up at the moon and see the racks of midnight driven masterless across its lunatic face, it is for us but a common vision. 'It is working up for rain,' we say, and our interests return at once to our own temporal affairs. Look again! The wraiths of mist that veil in their flight that sphere so wod and wan are unshepherded, and it is beneath such tattered banners of casualty that the populations kiss each other's wayward flesh, crying out each upon the other, till the hour when in an unbroken silence their corpses, short and long, await their burial.

We walked down the wide street. I made Dittany turn to see how Montacute Hill appeared on the horizon in exact line with the ancient road, almost as if the road had been planned deliberately to secure a view of the shapely hill. Indeed, Montacute Hill must have been a familiar daily landmark to Roger Bacon, not only in sunny summer weather, but also when dun-coloured snow-clouds, blowing southward from Bristol, rushed darkly over the protecting eminence of the quiet village.

Polden Hills are picking their geese
Faster, faster, faster !

I took Dittany into the Dolphin. I had a gin and milk and she some ginger-beer out of a glass bottle with an

Adam's apple in its throat. It was the same sort of bottle that the men used to drink out of on Club Days, and also the bandsmen at School-Treats, after the rogues, 'with their bones covered four fingers thick with good Christian fat,' had set every man and maid in Bishopston and the Borough tapping heel and toe to hear once again their Kingsbury jig.

> *Carter for Mister Manley*
> *He worked at Wulham's Mill*
> *And up by barton and down by mead*
> *He sang to the maidens upon his reed.*
> *' Apples be ripe,' he sang to them !*
> *' And nuts be brown,' they answered him.*

I tried to persuade Dittany to taste my gin and milk, but she would not. It was exciting to me to be with her in a public-house. It seemed to suggest a future when we might be free in the world together. We sat side by side. The room was bare and smelt of cider, stale tobacco, and the sweat of farm labourers fresh in from pitching and tedding hay.

' Well, 'tis proper hot and no mistake,' the landlord remarked as he put down the glasses before us. ' And we can do with a dab of het till the meads be carried, though it do make man and maid sweaty and no doubt about it.' When he had gone out Dittany showed her amusement, opening her eyes very wide after her manner. She evidently relished the sight of this large man moving about in his shirt-sleeves taking all the world for granted, and swallowing it with a gulp as a fish swallows a gnat. As for me, I liked well to think of all flesh sweltering under the June sky, horses rubbing sweaty flanks between the shafts of haycarts, cattle standing on patches of grassless ditch dust under hedges, labourers working without coats in every field, girls in ivy-green, sparrow-chirping dairies turning cheeses, and children coming back from school as freckled as eggs. Dittany had already a brown skin, had become what used to be called 'a summer tanling,' and looked as though in her heart she was now, very now, singing the old lines :

> Whatever they say, this be the day ;
> I must love.
> Over there in the meadow hay—
> I want love, this be the day——

We walked to the bridge. Below us flowed the river Yeo. We could see fish in a pool near one of the buttresses, facing up-stream and almost motionless. Dittany admired the river-weeds, whose long green streamers waved and swayed in the current. ' If *you* weren't here to make love to me I would like a river god to take me into his arms to-day and carry me to some rushy couch.' I liked her

134

imagining and did not like it. Though the fox run, the chicken hath wings. Surely she was such another as the Greek girl who fell in love with a river not far from her father's threshold, and, through perfidy, suffered the strong embraces of Poseidon himself, instead of those of her first true love, of the first of her silver paramours.

' She loved a river, far the fairest of the floods that run upon the earth. And it came to pass that the girdler of the world, the Earth-shaker, put on the shape of the river, and lay by the lady at the mouth of the whirling stream. Then the dark wave stood around them like a hill-side bowed, and hid the God and the mortal woman. And he undid her maiden girdle.'

Dittany's white arm was resting on the parapet. I touched it, her elbow was as cold as a dawn mushroom. ' It is just the arm of an ordinary girl,' I thought. A dog's nose and a woman's elbow are always cold. Probably within a radius of five miles there are fifty girls who would have funny-bones just as chill and charming as hers, so that if they were all of them resting side by side on the stone coping of Ilchester Bridge, it would be a job to tell which was which of the hundred crooked forearms. In what then did my infatuation lie ? I remembered having been told by a friend of a romantic love ditty

135

which he had heard a young Neapolitan girl sing in a dance-hall at Taormina. She sang, he told me, like a nightingale alone in a poplar grove and, indeed, pressed so much quivering passion into her voice that the audience of rude vineyard-pruning Latin lubies completely lost their heads and ran lunatic with lust. Was my feeling for Dittany at bottom the same ? She seemed to float above me always intangible as a cloud, as a mist above a water-meadow, as a song in an attic. With a sudden drop of my spirits my thought took now a fresh turn. Very likely her love for me was not so very deep. She was like a butterfly sunning itself on a hot stone, opening and folding its painted wings. To be loved was what mattered to her and not by whom !

I am dark and fair to see,
Young in my virginity,
Rose my colour is and white,
Pretty mouth and green my eyes ;
And my breast it pricks me so
I may not endure it,
For I meddle me to know
Love, and naught can cure it.

Whenever thoughts of this kind entered my head I was at once dejected. I knew that if I came to any deep, real mistrust of Dittany I would be ready to curse life itself. My mind could be firm and gallant in its approach to everything except what had to do with her. Wherever she might be concerned I would hate an evil truth. I never wanted to hear such truth spoken or to see such truth written. I wanted to die faithful, believing a lie.

> *Under this stone,*
> *In gloom and darkness vast,*
> *Lies the green lover,*
> *Faithful to the last.*

'Wouldn't it be lovely,' she said, 'if we could get a boat and go down the river?' I didn't for a moment suppose that it would be possible to gratify her whim, but I saw an old woman in a white sun-bonnet standing by her latch-gate, and thought I would talk to her.

I never forgot the scene as I approached the cottage; it has remained with me all my life. There was this little aged woman out of the old world looking up the road from the security of her narrow red-brick path, surrounded by a blaze of summer flowers; by scarlet geraniums, by drowsy heavy-headed peonies, by lupins and larkspurs and hollyhocks, and above all by those parti-coloured pinks which the Elizabethans were used to call sops-in-wine and that were 'worne of Paramoures.' I have always admired those simple parish almanacs that in the brightest colours represent such gardens. Pictures of the same kind are sometimes to be seen in seed merchants' catalogues, and always they reassure me, suggesting, as they do, a life that is slow-moving and solid, a matter-of-fact life of busy honey-bees in midsummer garden plots, of wasps humming against parlour window frames.

This day the sunne is in his chieftest hight,
With Barnaby the bright.

The strong meridian sunshine pressed down upon the chimney-pots of the old town, upon the dusty flanks of snoring farmyard swine grumbling in straw ; upon back-door buckets, upon rusting hinges, and thumb-polished rural latches. In just such a firm flower-bordered world as that of the almanacs did I seem to be alive and about that day, a world as innocent as it was thick, a world basking for ever secure and jocund under the light of the countenance of a lion-and-unicorn-God as by law estab-lished. I was supremely happy. I did not forget the gladness of the life I had led ever since my childhood, but with my love for Dittany I felt I had stepped sud-denly into a new life, or, at any rate, had had some radiant intensity wonderfully superimposed upon my known days.

The old woman proved to be as deaf as any of her flower-pots. For a long time I could not make her understand a single word. As soon as she did catch at my meaning she began explaining that she herself had a boat at the bottom of her kitchen-garden behind the old house. It belonged, she explained, to her son, who used it for the duck shooting in the winter when the floods were out. But he had been away all that summer and she doubted whether the boat was not full of water. I could look at it. I called to Dittany, but she remained leaning over the parapet of the bridge, evidently deep sunk in one of her dreaming moods. I hurried back to the bridge to fetch her. She was elated at hearing of my success. It was all very much to her mind, the incomparable sunshine, the old lady, the coolness of the stone-flagged passage along which we had to pass in order to reach the back garden with its motionless rows of broad-beans and long borders of southernwood or lad's love growing on each side of the path.

> Lad's Love is lassies' delight
> And if lads won't love, lassies will flite.

As we approached the river, at the garden's lower end the neat orderliness gave place to a jungle of artichokes, that rose high as palms above a wealth of luxurious rhubarb leaves whose damp, broad-spreading foliage must have provided even in the warmest weather unseen areas of dampness and shadow for the pasturing of insatiable slime-slippery slugs. In the middle of this green vegetable forest stood an ancient tree the branches of which were leaning directly over the water. 'What is that?' I asked, not recognizing the growth of the tree whose fruit commemorates the tragedy of the Babylonian lovers dead three thousand years ago. I had to repeat my question. 'It is a mulberry,' the old woman said. 'My father used to tell me that my grandfather planted it the day the stage-coach brought the news of the Battle of Waterloo to Pye Corner. It still fruits very well,' she continued. 'I sugar some every year for Christmas, my son likes to eat them that way. 'Tis a fancy of his.'

She led us to the water's edge. It was not the main river but a kind of back stream. The bottom of the boat, as she had anticipated, was full of water. 'I'll get you something to bail the water out with,' she said, and began hurrying back up the path. Dittany was quick to follow her and I saw a sleek white cat spring on to the path in front of them. It had been sleeping unseen in the shade of a row of spinach. I climbed into the boat and, finding a tin, began dipping at the bilge-water. My mind was overflowing with feelings of pure delight. Sunshine possessed me. How grateful I was to be alive! Gertrude and Bertie had laughed at me once when in the schoolroom as a child, on an autumn evening, working at my cross-stitch under the yellow light of the lamp, I unexpectedly exclaimed, 'I do love you, Miss Beales.' It was, I suppose, a sudden overwhelming sense of well-being that prompted the thoughtless utterance, for even then the sense of existence would suddenly fill me with exultation so that I could have lifted up my head and crowed like a cock a dozen times in the day. So besotted was I by the gift of consciousness that even to open the schoolroom cupboard with its odd smell, to get out my pencil-box and pot-hook copybook, would make me exclaim with gladness. All life was then a pleasure. It was a pleasure to have the lessons interrupted by my mother coming in to look after her tame white dove strutting over the sandy floor of its roomy cage with its pink feet. It was a pleasure to learn the poem Words-worth wrote to a kitten playing with leaves, or the poem by William Allingham that begins 'Up the airy moun-tains,' and then later, in the schoolroom-walk for Katie and me to be shown by Miss Beales polychrome Columkill lights in the froth bubbles at the edge of the pool below the heavily revolving water-wheel of the Montacute Mill.

Dittany took a little time, but when at last she did appear, coming down the path, she was carrying a kitchen stoup like the one that Mrs. Goddard used for peeling potatoes. With this utensil I was able to work much more quickly, especially as Dittany also began bailing with the old cocoa-tin I had discarded.

'You have no idea,' she said, 'what a wonderful old woman she is. It is as if the witch in the lilac cottage had told us just what was going to happen, told us to go to an old woman who would be standing outside her house on the Northover side of the Ilchester Bridge. Her rooms are full of the most wonderful treasures. She has a pin-cushion with old lace round it and pins arranged to make the words "Welcome little stranger." She told me the pins had been put into place a month before she was born and they had been kept like that ever since.'

I went on with my bailing in silence, but my mind was full of the strangeness of birth, of the mystery of how human beings each in their generation are summoned into 'the coasts of light.' How extraordinary it seemed that life should be able to call up life out of the abyss of nothingness ; that a boy and girl lying together in a physical transport should be able to summon to the earth a new soul, and that this fresh soul, free as a migratory bird, should in due time, by the same sublime process, create yet another. By such a series of common miracles Death really is deprived of half his victory, for how could he not balk to see man's silver seed for ever sustaining mortal life against his never-ending strokes ?

When all was ready I paddled the boat out of the back-water into the big river. Dittany sat in the stern of our craft and directed our course with a long thin rudder handle of a kind I had never seen before. With the greatest pride we glided gently and silently over the deep pool where we had watched the fish, and underneath one of the dark cool arches of the ancient bridge.

16

*Be not ignorant of this one thing, that one day is with
the Lord as a thousand years, and a thousand years as
one day.*

ANCIENT WISDOM

IN THE FREE RANGE OF MY MEMORY I WAS WITH THOSE
' whose feet do tread green paths of youth and love,'
drifting with Dittany on the broad back of the idle
Yeo out from under the round shadows into reaches, with
levels of sunshine-water shimmering between two high
butterfly banks thick-grown with long purples, mimulus,
water avens, cool comfrey, and light, trailing hay-seed
grasses, but my real condition was far otherwise. In my
mind's eye actual as shoe leather, I saw it all again, the
shining waterway of the river ; the flashing dragon-flies,
and above our glad heads that knew not one grey hair,
the spacious firmament with swallows sharking after the
flies through the hot atmosphere of a planet that smelt of
all the foison of midsummer. Meanwhile, in the wedge
of the clamping reality in which I was trying to catch
my breath my mutinous body pressed for attention. Its
insistence was terrifying to me. The mind is quick, the

144

mind is clamouring still for life and more life, and lo! the secret servants of the material creature, those myriad subject servants who for so long a period have ministered to a man's well-being, deftly healing the hand scratched by the mischief of a thorn, controlling with inspired ingenuity the mysteries of metabolism, swift to devise warning signals at the first indication of physical mal-adjustment, suddenly rebel, and, in a twinkling, have been transformed into a rout of absconding abjects, faltering and irresolute, with panic treacherously conspiring to drag the haughty spirit down to the dust.

I would think that the bleeding was stopping, but then suddenly it would begin again, as impossible to prevent as the overflow from a leaking cistern. It was in the early morning, the hour when cats run home, and badgers shuffle themselves into their sets, and I was looking across at the cattle on Chaldon Down opposite. It was one of those August mornings that presage the autumn ; the mist and the dew and the spider webs were as one. My night nurse had silently disappeared and her place had been taken by my brother Bertie. He sat by my side with his fine Roman head sensitively solicitous ; for our affec-tions were bound together by unbreakable bonds. We had always been companions. As boys we had been sent back to bed by my father because we were out on the lawn at three o'clock on a summer morning ; as a boy, with

LOVE AND DEATH

him at my side, I had hammered my fingers driving nails
into the Mabelulu roof ; as boys we had found a haw-
finch's nest, as boys balanced ourselves on stilts ; and as
boys had been reluctantly coerced into playing cricket
at Norton for the Montacute Third Eleven ! His head
as I looked at it evoked countless memories. It was a
head that suggested force of character, but at the same
time extreme vulnerability. It made him nervous to see
me so ill. The blood began to flow and soon I was once
more struggling against suffocation. Although fully
aware of the damage that they might do I was impotent
against the spasms of violent coughing.

The hæmorrhage, however, ended at last, leaving me
still alive though much weaker than before. An old oak
is not fell'd with one chop. Again I lay back, grateful
for even a precarious respite. To recover serenity enough
to continue my reveries, to continue filching happiness
from out of the store-house of my memories, it was
necessary for me to rally and to pacify my craven senses.
The beauty of the morning did slowly restore me to a
condition of calm. I watched our cat Lupe stalking a
robin, creeping between our newly planted winter-greens
with its belly close upon the ground. More than anything its demoniac concentration made me realize my
inconsequence in Nature's unresting procedures. With
the same implicit obedience the distant cows were swing-

146

ing their tails. If I died it was no matter. Montaigne in his essay declares that in the hour of death Nature instructs how best to conduct oneself. Anyhow, my agony was not yet, and as Epicurus and Shakespeare had taught, when once I was dead I certainly would have nothing more to fear. With such simple windfalls of thought I slowly regained my composure and, in fact, for several hours was once more completely happy in my memories of that love 'which reachest but to dust.'

17

Still, though none should hark again,
Drones the blue-fly in the pane.

.   .   .   .   .

Floats the boat that is forgot
None the less to Camelot.

EDNA ST. VINCENT MILLAY

OUT OF THE DARK SHADOW OF THE BRIDGE WE
passed upon the shining dolphin-back of the
river of Life. Dittany took her task of steering
seriously, watching the course of the boat with responsible
care. I made up my mind to row as far as Pill Bridge.
Pill Bridge is a narrow pack-bridge that my brother
Willie had shown me once when we had walked along
the bank of the Yeo from his ivy-walled dairy farm near
Ash. As I rowed I looked at Dittany. Her cheeks were
flushed from the sun. I had never in my life seen any
girl look more utterly desirable than she did. It would
be impossible to tell how perfect she was that day. Never
with words could I hope to recapture that passing appearance of her pure beauty, a silent, shadowed beauty like
a bird's in a leafy hedge. As delicate and mysterious
she looked as the lady-fern when it first opens in the

148

depth of a green-foliaged copse, its seeds all in place, those minute seeds on the under side of its fronds which it was once believed, if swallowed, would enable a lover to visit the bedchamber of his sweetheart unseen. Whether she lay under sparrow-hollowed thatch, or beneath leaded roofs ' bosom'd high in tufted trees,' with such a diet of 'hundreds and thousands' in his belly it was all one, and he would surely see his darling in her naked unaffrighted retirement before the next sunrise. Dittany resembled just such a withdrawn fern, the timidest of the forest and the most full of magical properties, and she also could be likened to a fawn standing near to its mother's dappled flank with wide-open eyes ; but she also was like a speckled thrush singing unseen in a late evening of February when the outsides of all the small blue folded-up petals of the first squills are soaked with rain.

I rowed very indolently. We were already far from Ilchester Bridge and alone in the wide fields. We passed a cornfield where the wheat was growing without a rustle in the blazing noon. The corn was tall but still bright green and with no ears yet topping each leafy spike. The sun was now very high up in a cloudless sky, and in the distance towards Kingston I could see cattle galloping ; evidently stung by gadflies. We watched a water-rat moving along its slippery causeway with fur as soft as a beaver's. Dittany was steering now with less anxiety.

She had settled herself into a more comfortable position.
I could see beneath her pretty rose frock where the sun
made a sharp line, and what a peerless pavilion was
present under this shadowed canopy, a pavilion whiter
and fresher far than a cherry branch when not one round
petal has fallen from its thin-stemmed multitudinous
flowers, nodding in tremulous equipoise against the
eye of an early morning. All that wonderful summer
day my body had kept asserting its love in one simple
insistent sentence. The poetry of life exalted my imagination. What I felt initiated into was a thicker and
more actual poetry than had ever been, or ever could be,
expressed by fretful words. I carried a volume of Landor
in my pocket, but what were his smooth classical verses
against the radiance of this day and against the flowing
water beneath us with its teeming inheritance of percep-
tible and imperceptible life ? As if she read my thoughts,
Dittany suddenly said, ' Llewelyn, say me some poetry.'
I was dashed by her request ; I never could remember
poetry. But the very spirit of the day brought these lines
to my mind :

> Only reapers, reaping early
> In among the bearded barley,
> Hear a song that echoes cheerly
> From the river winding clearly,
>   Down to tower'd Camelot.

The simple schoolroom-lines seemed to satisfy Dittany. Nero was said to trawl for fish with a golden net, and poetry was always the golden net by which Dittany could be most easily enmeshed. She would remain motionless, all sensitive attention, listening and listening like a hare at pause in her hedgerow meuse. I told her how I remembered quite clearly seeing pictures of Tennyson's funeral in the *London Illustrated News*, a child of eight at my mother's side on the red dining-room sofa.

We drifted on. Sometimes the river-banks were so high that I could not see above them. We reached Pill Bridge at last, and floated under one of its narrow arches. When we rounded the next bend we found that the river was divided into two by an island with willow and alder-trees growing on it. ' Oh! do let us stop here! ' Dittany cried. I took two or three hard pulls at the oars and drove the boat right through the rushes till its prow with a thud struck solid ground. We shipped the oars and got out, but we had no rope to tie up the boat with. In a moment Dittany had taken off her sash and slipping one end of it through an iron ring that hung at the boat's front had fastened it to a willow-bough. ' Why should I be afraid to lose my girdle when there is nobody here but you ? ' she laughed. The marrow inside my bones took fire at her words.

Give me but what this ribband bound,
Take all the rest the sun goes round !

I threw my arms about her, kissing her and kissing her.
She felt my love, I knew it. Her eyes shone, as the eyes
of an inexperienced girl who is startled by the very
violence of the passion she has roused. The island, we
discovered, was much larger than we had first thought.
In its centre was a small lawn, ' a moist river lawn,'
though, in the blaze of that fine summer, russet-dry enough.
This lawn was surrounded by willow-trees against the
trunks of which driftwood and water litter, washed down
in the winter floods, had become lodged. The little green
sward had evidently been just above the level of the
turgid deluge. As we came on to it we saw a moor-hen
hurry away into the encircling forest of rushes which stood
so high that as soon as we lay down we were completely
hidden from view even from the top of the river-flood
banks. With vexing perversity Dittany now wanted me
to read Landor to her. I could not bear to do this.
However, as it grew clear to me she had set her heart
upon the folly and would not be content till I had gratified her wish, I submitted. I turned over the leaves and
began :

An ancient chestnut's blossoms threw
Their heavy odour over two :

Leucippe, it is said, was one ;
The other, then, was Alciphron.
' Come, come ! why should we stand beneath
This hollow tree's unwholesome breath ? '
Said Alciphron, ' here's not a blade
Of grass or moss, and scanty shade.
Come ; it is just the hour to rove
In the lone dingle shepherds love ;
There, straight and tall, the hazel twig
Divides the crookèd rock-held fig,
O'er the blue pebbles where the rill
In winter runs and may run still.
Come then, while fresh and calm the air,
And while the shepherds are not there.'

LEUCIPPE.   *But I would rather go when they*
Sit round about and sing and play.
Then why so hurry me ? for you
Like play and song, and shepherds too.

ALCIPHRON.   *I like the shepherds very well,*
And song and play, as you can tell.
But there is play, I sadly fear,
And song I would not have you hear.

LEUCIPPE.   *What can it be ? What can it be ?*

ALCIPHRON.   *To you may none of them repeat*
The play that you have play'd with me,
The song that made your bosom beat.

153

LEUCIPPE.   *Don't keep your arm about my waist.*
ALCIPHRON. *Might you not stumble?*
LEUCIPPE.   *Well then, do.*
                 But why are we in all this haste?
ALCIPHRON. *To sing.*
LEUCIPPE.   *Alas! and not play too?*

She was ready now, but she still would not allow me to possess her utterly, and unless she was happy I was not happy. To see a shadow of misgiving pass across her face was enough to spoil all :

> *With margerain gentle,*
> *The flower of goodlihead,*
> *Embroidered the mantle*
> *Is of your maidenhead.*

Our love that day had still to be but the love of children, and yet how charming to be so occupied in such a secret place. It was as though a honey-bee were lightly rifling fuchsia flowers of their sun-warmed peculiar window-sill honey, flowers whose sweets were protected so daintily. Everything she was wearing captivated me. To see and to touch what had been next to her naked body was alone enough to render me as apt and fain as a chanticleer on a fair day.

Our shoes are made of leather,
Our stockings are made of silk,
Our pinafores are made of calico,
As white as any milk.

I was so happy, so ardent, so inebriate with the contacts of our flesh that my infatuated consciousness could catch only fleeting glimpses of her as she was in her entire identity. The smell of her body was like mowing-machine grass hot in the sun, just as sweet, just as healthy, and yet touched with an animal rankness too, a ground-ivy rankness that made my blood race and race again. Surely she was made of a most precious clay.

Yet the glimpses that I did get of her, bare as a birch, in the midst of my transport remained sharply imprinted upon my mind—the smoothness of her back with the movement of her shoulder-blades so subtly visible, her feet so precisely furnished with toes, each of them tipped with shining pink shells of civil horn! How pale she looked against the green of the grass, this Naiad of the Yeo, this child-like far-strayed Oread!

No beauty she doth miss
When all her robes are on :
But Beauty's self she is
When all her robes are gone.

155

I am sure that day she did love me truly. She said sweet things I have never forgotten. It would have been impossible, I think, to match her cool breasts with their pretty points projecting from each pap, magnolia-white. All the marvel, and all the glory of life that had ever been upon earth seemed to me to have become pressed into the wonder of her body ; than to be allowed to lie in her arms and forget everything, I could not imagine a rarer chance. It was impossible to believe that any other girl of her age could give pleasure as she gave it, pleasure

Whose fruits none rightly can describe, but he
That pulls or shakes it from the golden tree.

Long, long I lay ensorcelled by her fairness. Her eyes were wide open, happy with love and with the knowledge of the empire she held over me. 'Tell me,' she said at last, 'Tell me *in words* why exactly you think me so beautiful.' Suddenly my head began to ring and ring again with ancestral voices, with the voices of ancient bards long since dead and I dared to answer her after their traditional manner ; so fiercely did my imagination respond to the inspiration of her nearness, and so rashly did I try to unburden my soul. 'The clustered purple of your hair is like the leaves of the incense-bearing Arabian tree within whose shadows the bird sings unseen to the dawn. Your eyes are twilight pools in the forest, shaded by the undersides of swaying branches, shivering and trembling in a soft moonlight. Your mouth is a dew-drenched hedge, garlanded with honeysuckle whose " flaunting beauty revels along upon the wind," and where the yearlings crop in regular rows, fresh and wool-white from the sheep-washing pool of the farm. Your ears are like a brace of quail that cower on each side of a fragrant stone, grown about with myrtle, and of their harbourage none know. Your back is a madonna lily silently standing with timid droop. Your arms long and small were shaped out of the flying sea-foam, out of the fair flesh of a myriad wood-anemones fluttering unheeded in moss-grown hollows. Your breasts are like twin Alpine peaks that pierce the celestial night, their slopes of frost, showing under the stars shadowless and immaculate. Your belly is a wide cows-leas white as snow with the daisies of April, and at its centre is the love-knot of the generations. Your strong knees are like unto twin stones of chalk at the sea's margin, large, rounded pebbles, polished by gleaming salt, and beyond belief pale in the languid hours of the lozel night. Your legs are straight and strong as two silver birch-trees. At the dividing place of them lies all the treasure of human kind.'

Presently I made a little path through the rushes for her

157

and we both went down into the water. She did not wish to get her hair wet so she tied her shift about her head. A kingfisher flashed by to settle upon a flood-post fifty yards down stream. We swam all round the island. I kept very close to her. I feared she might vanish, drown, or return to her playmates of the river, diving suddenly out of sight, with never a word spoken.

> *' Ye wash, ye wash, ye bonny may,*
> *And ay's ye wash your sark o' silk.—*
> *' It's a' for ye, you gentle knight,*
> *My skin is whiter than the milk.'*

It was so hot, with the sun warming for our tread every waterside stone and pebble, that she was in no hurry to put her clothes on. When she did begin to dress she snatched at her frock to cover herself while she adjusted her buttons and laces.

> *Around a green gravel*
> *The grass was so green,*
> *And all the fine ladies*
> *Ashamed to be seen.*

Presently we both were sitting opposite each other eating our luncheon, eating what remained of our egg sand-wiches and sponge-cakes and raisins. ' Think that there are people who would call us immoral for playing as we have done,' I said.—'Only wicked people could think in that way,' she said. 'How many kisses have you given me to-day from the beginning? They must have been a hundred, and yet I remember every one,' she said. After we had satisfied our hunger I unknotted her hair and it fell over her shoulders. She was wearing a small round brooch no bigger than a shilling and set about with thirteen faded turquoises. Except for a necklace of coral this was the only ornament she ever wore and I had been touched to see this nursery jewel carefully pinned upon her folded clothes when we came up from the river through the rushes after our bathe, her wet feet, as white as sleet, indenting the damp mud.

I used often to wish that we could be dull so that the hours we spent together would go more slowly. Our natures were so consonant the one with the other that whenever we met our beings seemed to engage in a kind of ecstatic dance, the whirling dance of birds in mid-air, or one like the love-dance of birds-of-paradise, whose feathers become all but invisible in the frenzy of their spinnings.

We threw away our honey and bread to the chub that were lurking in the deep holes under the roots of the island willows.

In my lover's arms
Soft pillowed,
Down by the willows, by the willows.

When I next took my watch out it was half-past five
and there were already long shadows under the meadow
hedges. I went to get the boat ready and then returned
to fetch her, grudging to let her be. I had in my hand
a large water-forget-me-not, and when I came upon her,
shy and embarrassed, I gave her the flower. It was an
occasion I always remembered afterwards. For suddenly
tears were in her eyes and she looked at me as if she
herself knew the future better than I, far better than I !
She fastened the flower to her frock with her turquoise
pin.

We returned slowly upstream, enjoying every odorous
breath of the damp soft summer evening. Everywhere
the fish were rising, now before us, now behind us, with
unexpected sparkling splashes. The birds were beginning
to sing again and the cattle, their milking over, were
moving about the fields, slowly, slowly, slowly, with their
great heads bowed close to the cool river-side grass. Each
sedgy stream that emptied its shallow waters into the river
emitted a breath warm and deep. From time to time
gentle evening winds moved across the flat fields, causing
the long grasses and the thinner reeds to bend and rustle.

We knew that after so hot a day the parched ground would presently be refreshed by a heavy fall of dew, with never rod, pole, or perch passed over by it throughout the royal shires. No wonder the roach and dace were feeding so greedily, for above the surface of the river flickered a population of gnats. In the wildest morris mazes they whirled, celebrating after the dizzy fashion of their tribe the passing of the longest day of the year.

At a turn of the river we saw a strange sight. The head of a black horse lifted itself suddenly above the raised flood-bank on our right. The animal looked at us and yawned, showing an ugly row of horse-teeth agape against the evening sky. The cart horse might have been the eight-hoofed stallion of Woden, so monstrous did it appear.

' It's a Water-kelpie,' Dittany called in great excitement. ' They are always seen near rivers and floods.'

' What is a Water-kelpie ? ' I asked.

The side was stey, and the bottom deep,
Frae bank to brae the water pouring;
And the bonny grey mare did sweat for fear,
For she heard the water-kelpy roaring.

I had held up the oars and allowed the boat to drift as it would, the better to hear her voice. She repeated the strange lines without raising her eyes from the waters of the Yeo. 'The Water-kelpie,' she explained, 'is an equine beast that haunts rivers, marshlands, and floods. If you are cunning it can be mastered with a halter made of hops twisted together with black briony. When once such a halter falls over a Water-kelpie's neck he will be gentle and can be led direct to the nearest stable. There are only three sounds to be feared when he is being so led —the hissing of a gander—the death-rattle of an old wife —and a maiden's cry for her lost virginity! If any of these noises reach a Water-kelpie's ears he'll break from his harness. Perhaps,' she continued, 'when King Lear spoke so snappishly of women, saying, "Down from the waist they are Centaurs, though women all above," he really meant to say down from the waist they are Water-kelpies. I wonder if you think that I have been a Water-kelpie down from my waist to-day?' She no longer trailed her hands in the river, but looked at me so seriously that I was touched. 'When people are in love,' I said, 'they have only to think how best they can give pleasure to each other. Nothing else should be in their heads. It is the happy dispensation of lovers, their private grace; and the more shameless and tameless the feelings they are able to excite the better are they obeying the will of the fairies.'

162

'Well, in any case,' said she, 'if you catch the Water-kelpie you have only the gander's hiss and the death-rattle to fear,' and she looked at me with eyes full of ambiguous implication.

18

And mark'd thee, when the stars come out and shine,
Through the long dewy grass more slow away.

MATTHEW ARNOLD

WHEN WE GOT BACK AND HAD SECURED THE BOAT and put the oars carefully away in the shed the old woman came out in a black Sunday dress saying that she had made some tea for us because she thought the young lady might be tired. We were conducted into her sitting-room and found that the meal had been all laid out in readiness against our return, with a cosy over the tea-pot and two eggs by the side of both of our plates. Dittany had evidently won the old woman's heart. The unobtrusive gentleness of her manners had always a charm. Her lack of any sort of aggressiveness was reassuring ; people at last found themselves in the presence of a creature without horns, or teeth, or claws, or kicking heels. She might have been a daughter of the house by the way she was now taken up stairs to wash her hands. The parlour where we sat was agreeable. China dogs and tropical shells were on the chimney-piece, and on one of the walls a coloured picture of Queen Victoria—an exact and solid image of the benevolent mother of all Englishmen. I did not know whether to pay or not : Dittany said she would arrange and I slipped money into her hand. However, the old woman would not take a penny. Dittany put up her head to be kissed and our hostess said good-bye to us at the door in a flutter of friendly animation. I do not forget even after so many years how dew-cool the garden smelt as we passed through it at the hour of twilight, that garden which had looked so dazzling bright in the heat of midday.

When we reached the top of Hunger Hill dusk had already fallen. Although the hours had slid by so swiftly it seemed to me as we neared the place where we had had breakfast as though an age had gone. How is it we can set no reliance upon the orderliness of our time-piece time ? In the measuring of periods of emotional experience this man-conceived astronomical method is essentially untrustworthy, and ' in this small course which birth draws out to death ' it is possible for the whole tally of a man's days to appear suddenly abbreviated to the span of a seaside holiday.

> *Had I loved but a day*
> *To all I'd say,*
> *' Sweet is love.'*

We came back by the fields. We passed over the plank where my brother John had predicted that one day we would both write books ; but my mind was not concerned with such matters now. Night had taken possession of Somerset. We might have been inhaling from the moist throat of some planetary ox. Voices from the village came pleasantly to our ears. A bark of a farmyard dog disturbed the quiet ; reassuring it sounded in its farmyard homeliness against the hushed spaces of the prodigal universe. As we walked together I showed Dittany the stars. Charlemagne's wain was before us and I taught her to find the little secondary star that forever accompanies the second large star of the waggon's shaft. I told her how in the desert the Arabs test the eyesight of their children by whether they can see it or not, that faint, faint star which ploughmen in England have so well named ' Jack-by-the-middle-horse.' After curry-combing heavy horse-limbs—mired and damp from the furrow—they cross from stable to cottage and they tell their children this name, tramping home through the farmyard puddles, ' the gilded puddle which beasts would cough at,' illumined by star-shine.

Dim and charmed indeed, were those Tintinhull lanes with midsummer-moon lovers clinging tranced to each other at every field gate. The footfalls we made together, walking hand in hand, were all prized by me.

Continually headlong beetles would blunder past us and away over the wayside hedge into grassy pastures whose every flower was moth-visited, and where hedge-hogs, with cold noses and damp thorny shoulders, foraged hungrily for meat through massy grass jungles under the lee light of the moon. How happy I was ! It had always seemed when Dittany and I were alone together as if the estranging, isolating barriers that separate human beings suddenly fell away, so that our spirits became united without effort as water is to water. Her very breathing was audible to me, so still was the air.

On we passed through the immortal night, like two long-separated souls at peace and reunited at last in the crepuscular spaces of Elysium. Often there would come to us hot puffs of air, sweet with the perfume of banks of bedstraw, and presently we would pass near some field-stream, so overgrown with tangled brambles, starred already with pale blackberry flowers, and the tall growths of budding willow-herb, soft and damp to the touch, that it was impossible to see the crinkling water to which, every night, foxes, badgers, rats, and mice would come to lap with parched tongues large and little ; and where, in the day, frogs would hop and small birds stand to dip and prink their sleek feathers—to fly away a moment later in freedom. When we reached the gate by the field of Wulham's Mill we got over it, walking a little into

the field where we began once again to kiss each other.
And how sweetly she could kiss ! Her kisses were the
wet kisses of a little girl, kisses that were in themselves
separate actions of tender love, kisses that were more
eloquent than words could have been of gentle surrenders,
passionate and true. I held her close in my arms :

> O ! thou art fairer than the evening air
> Clad in the beauty of a thousand stars.

At our feet the dewdrops were glistening like to the island
galaxies of the astral universe above our two heads. The
moonshine on the wet meadow, the moonshine that was
everywhere present in the airy levels of the night sky,
was of so pellucid an essence that it penetrated to each
morsel of matter that grew, crawled, or flew among those
sequestered fields. It glinted upon the myriad herbs that
had on them the coldness of the night. It tipped the moist
horns of each voyaging snail with its pale sheen ; and the
furry coats and flickering leather wings of every bat were
miraculously silvered, as these goblin beings, so shrill of
voice, circled in quaint Barnaby measures above us. It
almost seemed as if some colony of white bats had arrived
from China intent upon making their homes on this
undisturbed parcel of English ground ; at night bestowing
upon the abeyant pastures and walled-in cottage patches
a hungry supervision, and in the daytime hanging in

somnolent suspension, like balls of ermine, in the apple attics or unused cheese-lofts of Wulham's Mill ; where, in a demi-darkness, bitch spiders with eight legs and bulging, unappeasable abdomens sat for hours awaiting with a patience, malicious and zealous, the significant shiverings of their dusty webs.

> *Ah ! strange were the dim, wide meadows,*
> *And strange was the cloud-strewn sky,*
> *And strange in the meadows the corn crakes,*
> *And they making cry !*

> *The hawthorn bloom was by us,*
> *Around us the breath of the south.*
> *White hawthorn, strange in the night-time—*
> *His kiss on my mouth !*

Some haymakers unexpectedly came down the lane and we moved beneath the shadow of a tall hedge-elm tree. The smell of cider reached us as we stood silent and motionless while the labourers passed. One of them was walking a little behind the other three. He was perhaps the most unsteady on his legs. He stopped opposite us. ' I see boogur,' he said slowly. After this exclamation he hurried on to overtake his mates. I was so amused by his exclamation that I whispered to Dittany that the man was as drunk ' as a sheep.' Chaucer, I said, often used the expression ' drunk as a mouse,' but the true mediæval differentiations of states of drunkenness were four in number. In the first stage of intoxication the merry-maker was described as being drunk as a sheep, that is to say, good-natured drunk ; in the second stage he was drunk as a lion, that is noisy ; in the third stage drunk as an ape, foolish ; and in the fourth stage to be drunk as a swine, sottish drunk. This was the very kind of information that as a rule would have caught Dittany's attention, but standing under the shadow of the hedge in that wide-moon-mead, a corncrake calling, she seemed utterly caught away in one of her translunar moods. I felt as if something unearthly had laid a finger on her cold mouth.

Come hald thy peace, thou foolish lass,
The moon's but glancing in thy eye.

19

'*Is it even so?*' *said my Lady.*
'*Even so!*' *said my Lord.*
From WALTER DE LA MARE'S *Anthology, Come Hither.*

WHEN I REACHED HOME I FOUND EVERYBODY HAD gone to bed except my mother. She was in the drawing-room reading Disraeli's *Literary Anec-dotes*. She was in one of her happiest humours. It was extraordinary how she kept her interest in reading when she had had my father to manage for so many years, and all of us to look after, the village affairs as well. She used to order a box of books each winter from Mudie's Library and I would often find her reading as she sewed under the warm light of the dining-room lamp, the glass bowl of which was held high up above the table by its gun-metal Corinthian pillar. It was in the evenings that her spirit would expand, as though she were one of those flowers that open only in night air. In the daytime if she went out she always chose to walk, if it were possible, under the shadows of trees. She shunned the brighter places, she retreated from what was 'cheerful.' Her knees bent to the moon rather than to the sun. As

171

children we used to have bible-reading after breakfast, gathering about her on the sofa like Christiana's infant train in the second part of *Pilgrim's Progress*. At the end of our reading we would often sing a hymn. I remember once, 'There we will gather at the river, the beautiful, beautiful river,' had been chosen, and my mother had led the chant with a wild waving of the hand. Afterwards in the garden my brother John said to me, 'I love to see Mother as she was just now. She might have been worshipping the Horse-headed Demeter on the banks of some Phrygian stream.'

That evening I drew my chair close up to hers and held her hand in mine, that refined hand, each rose-tinged knuckle-line wrinkle of which I knew so well. 'I hope you have had a happy day, Llewelyn,' she said. 'A very happy day,' I answered, and I told her about going down the river and the old woman and the tea she had given us. 'A young girl's heart is a very tender thing,' she said after my story was over. 'You must be careful not to hurt or to betray it.' I longed to tell her of my love for Dittany and of my fear of losing her, and of how I could think of nothing else in the world but my love. I hesitated. The old French drawing-room clock beat out the minutes as the long hand rose in scarcely visible jerks towards the midnight hour. I remained dumb. It was as though the wings of time were brushing across that sheltered parlour of the Victorian age. I thought of my father sitting in his armchair occupied with his netting through the long winter evenings while my mother read to him, one after the other, the Waverley Novels, and I knew that his days would pass. I thought of Littleton looking over his camphor-smelling drawers of bright butterflies or when older reading *Endymion*, and of little Lucy, and I knew that their days would pass. I thought of John in summer weather with his long fingers stained with ink, writing at the same window, and how I had once run up to him as a small boy saying, ' How can you sit writing all the morning and not come out into the garden to play ? ' and I knew that his days would pass. And yet how permanent the room looked that evening, every picture, every print, every ornament part of my very conception of home— the tiger-skin rug, the bear-skin rug, the round polished table, the ottoman, the old family firescreens from Stalbridge ! I had hidden in this room when we had been playing at hide-and-seek in the Christmas holidays, and in the darkness, under the table, with the smell of the dust from the long black hair of the bear-skin rug in my nose, even as a very infant I had been aware of eternity ! In springtime, when the summer curtains were first hung, how incredibly loud the sound of the birds would be in the room as soon as ever the top sash of the window was put up.

It was as though my mother had followed my thoughts, for she suddenly said, 'Lulu, I have been reading in this old book of so many people who are now dead. Always after the story comes the word 'died,' and then a date ; 'died,' and then another date ; and it seems strange that my brother and my four sisters and myself should all be still alive and yet the year of my own death cannot be far away, the years of all of our deaths.'

In actual fact, her death came to her at the end of July, 1914. When she knew she was dying she called to my brother Bertie to carry her into the spare-room so that my father's night's rest should not be disturbed. She did not wish that the husband she had served so faithfully, bearing for him eleven children, should be incommoded by her death-agony. What errant thoughts she could harbour in her mind and how she loved all that was derelict, forlorn ; resenting as though by some inner mandate natural to her, all that was well-constituted, and illustrious ! Often when I was in bed and not asleep I have listened to her tired footsteps as they moved along the passages, seeing that all was in order, before herself going to bed ; entering empty rooms, the dressing-room perhaps, and opening and shutting drawers for no apparent reason. As my life-loving philosophy grew more and more part and parcel of my thoughts, I became aware of a definite antagonism between us, so wilful did her

dolorous attitude seem, for ever dwelling beyond all
reason upon the woes of the world. I even recollect on
one occasion deliberately ' making the fig ' in the direction
of her dragging steps outside my door, wishing my own
mother dead. When she did die I recalled what I had
done with a disturbing sense of remorse and was indeed
so troubled about it that I was innocent enough to take
my brother Theodore into my confidence. With an
irony characteristic of his mordant genius, he attempted
to lighten my misgivings. ' It is a matter of no con-
sequence,' he said. ' Why, if the truth were known, we
all of us are always wishing each other dead every day,
every hour of our lives.'

There was a bowl full of roses on the writing-table near
the silver inkstand and its flowers filled the whole room
with a haunting fragrance. The parlour with its oil paint-
ing of William Tell's chapel was eloquent of nineteenth-
century security. It was difficult to believe that the firm
family life of Montacute Vicarage was settled upon an
uncertain reef of quick-sand, in the midst of abrading
time currents. I had known nothing but this notable
island of domesticity. We had dwelt upon it all our lives :
and yet I have lived to see the house in the hands of
strangers, lived to come upon the old family three-wheeled
perambulator derelict amongst the fir-trees which my
father had planted to shelter the garden jakes.

My mother rose presently, and undoing the shutters stood gazing out into the embalmed darkness of the summer garden. It was the moon she wished to look at. It was high in the heavens. 'How beautiful thou art ! The world how deep !' Often had I watched my mother gaze out at the moon like this. On still summer evenings, and on wild autumn evenings when the branches of the old acacia swayed and creaked as the winds struck against them. 'The women knead their dough to make cakes for the Queen of Heaven,' or perhaps with some spiritual incantation she wished to draw the moon down to her, as the women of Thessaly were rumoured to be able to do. I have known her to stand in silence for a quarter of an hour to watch the planet race past the clouds far up above the Montacute House drive.

When her vigil was over and the hinged double shutters were once more closed she mentioned that my sister Gertrude had made up my bed in the Terrace-Walk and had put up my new tent over it. She said she felt uneasy about my sleeping out of doors and begged me for this one night at least to stay as usual in the nursery. But as soon as ever I understood that the tent was up, nothing could stop me from sleeping under it. When I was ready my mother heard my steps on the stairs and came to the back-door with a candle. I kissed her anxious forehead, and went out into the little yard.

It was the first time I had ever slept in the garden and this alone was sufficient to excite me. I opened up the tent so that I could see the full moon. Images of Dittany kept returning to my mind.

O Love ! they wrong thee much
That say thy sweet is bitter,
When thy rich fruit is such
As nothing can be sweeter.

I saw her again in Marsh Lane shaking hands with me in her odd, old-fashioned way. I saw her tying up the boat with her blue childish sash. I saw the grace of her swimming. I saw her lying face downwards watching with eager attention the fish as they idly dozed in the dark water below. The summer winds played gently through the trees, strong enough to sway the roosting birds, but not strong enough to lift their feathers. Far up above the paths and lawns, above each cool open rose-alley of the garden, hung the moon. ' By whispering windes soon lull'd asleep,' my day-dreams mingled presently with my night-dreams. They were difficult to separate and often I could not tell whether I had been sleeping or waking.

I dreamèd fast of mirth and play :
In youth is pleasure, in youth is pleasure.

177

I was walking along a grassy path between massed acres of royal fern, just such another fly-murmuring moorland track as that which leads through the bracken from Puddletown to the white gate at the back of the Hardy cottage at the end of Upper Bockhampton Lane. The dew of the dawn shone upon the turf bright as crystal. In my dream I saw Dittany at the end of an opening standing on a plot of grass below a cherry-tree in full blossom. We ran to meet each other, jubilant to kiss once more.

In my face 'tis written plain
How much I love her,
You who live in loving wise
There awaits you Paradise.

She was wearing her white dress fresh from the wash-tub. We walked away together hand in hand. We crossed a glade floored with rest-harrow and butterfly orchids. We passed through a forest where the singing of the small birds was so loud that we could hardly believe them to be birds. A unicorn, she told me, had been grazing on the smooth lawn. She showed me that the damp grass was everywhere marked with the indents of his sharp hoofs different entirely from the abatures of a stag, and that there were little heaps of grass-smelling dung like goat's dung, but dropped in pyramidic piles.

We reached the lonely cottage on ' Whistley Green' and

went up to the top room. Her bed had been prepared, our bed.

There blossomed suddenly a magic bed
Of sacred dittany and poppies red.

The sheets had been woven with the soft wool of dandelion clocks. 'It is to show us how different *our* time is from earth-time,' she said. 'When we are together here we live always by dandelion time.'

Now speak to me, blankets, and speak to me, bed,
And speak, then sheet, enchanted web.

I looked out of an open under-thatch window upon a seaside valley wooded with small spinneys of hawthorn trees, white with blossom ; and beyond these uplifted snowy acres I could see chalk cliffs and the sea, blue as the sky, against which a flock of snow-white gulls were flying. Birds were still singing, never did their ditties stop. 'What voices are those I hear in the valley ?' I asked.—'They are the voices of two children, the little girl with hair like mine, the boy with hair that gleams in the morning and is corn-coloured like yours.'— 'What are they doing out there ?' 'Now that you hear their shouts and laughter they fly together over the watery fields, and as they run they leap over the marsh-marigold-traced runnels to follow the clouded-yellows' fluttering

179

passage in from the sea, to follow them till they can mark where they have settled on flea--bane, or meadow-sweet, or Queen-Anne-lace.' With flushed cheeks and eyes of amethyst Dittany stood before me, more lovely than Guenever.

With a heart over-charged I once more looked out through the low-shadowed cottage window. A large red fox-hound was standing stock still in the tall flowering grasses with great grave eyes fixed upon me. 'It is my hound,' she said. 'I will show you all in the evening when the daisies are closing and the dew begins to fall. Over the watercress-bed that lies below in the hollow, where the prickly teasles grow, there is a reed-warbler's nest which, lightly as an Ariel's hammock, swings between four green rushes. I will show you all, all the wonders of Whistley Green, for time is long here,— but afterwards, let it be afterwards, not now.

> *Then did she doff the silken gown she wore*
> *And they began again their love of yore.*

20

A jealous man's horns hang in his eyes.

PROVERB

SHE HAD TOLD ME WHEN WE HAD PARTED BY HER white gates where the great oak tree stood that we could not see each other again for four days. Her mother was not well and she did not like to be long away from her. These four days taken from us in the very height of the hay-making time seemed to me a grievous loss. Golden dreams make men awake hungry. Mornings and afternoons now did not appear worth a farthing to me unless we were together.

After luncheon on the second afternoon my mother was reading to me when Mary Hockey came round the corner of the kitchen-garden path. She told us there was a young gentleman at the front door. She had his calling-card in the hot palm of her workaday hand. Mary Hockey's complete lack of any knowledge of ceremonious behaviour which so delighted my brother John and was in no way discouraged by my mother, was to me a continual cause of mortification. I was young and had not been long down from Cambridge where my mind

181

had become spoiled with conventional values. I felt offended to see the stranger's calling-card crumpled up in the girl's honest fist, especially when I discovered that it belonged to Randal Pixley. I told Mary to go back and to bring the gentleman down to us in the Terrace-Walk. My mother immediately got up from her garden chair with a look of ill-concealed impatience. She said she did not feel like receiving visitors that afternoon, and she would return to the house by the back way. As proud come behind as before. This characteristic flight on my mother's part pleased me as little as the crushed calling-card had done and I watched her figure turn the corner by the yew-tree with no very friendly eye. 'In reality,' I thought, ' she is as proud as Mary the Mother of God, and with her Shetland shawl held over her head, she only pretends to be humble, only pretends to be like the Montacute cottage women.' Our reading had not been as harmonious as usual that afternoon. We were in the middle of *De Profundis* and the supercilious style of the book with its elegant insincerities had provoked my mother. 'I do not object to the way Thomas Hardy writes of religion,' she had said ; ' his tone is always serious and dignified.' She had been won to Thomas Hardy by having read *Tess* in snatches from my own volume after the Mothers' Meeting in the schoolroom, for I had left the book on the shelf there. She had an interest in Wilde because she had once attended a lecture by him in Dorchester ; but this slight association was not strong enough to counteract the instinctive mistrust she felt of him.

My mother had hardly disappeared when round the corner by the fernery came Mary, followed by Mr. Pixley. I got up and took a few steps along the terrace to meet him. 'I beg you not to move,' he cried, raising a civil deprecating hand. I felt as attracted to him as I had been at The Grange. He was not strikingly good-looking, but his presence was distinguished. You knew that there was some essential fineness in him and a native humanity. This feeling I had for him was strengthened by my appreciation of his body. His build was slender and I always got the impression that the flesh that covered his lightly moving bones was as healthy as seaside winds. He sat down upon my mother's empty chair. Looking about him with content, he began praising the sound of the wood-pigeons from our deep orchards and I told him how our sister Philippa, the poet, hated that sound which to her suggested all that is smug, complacent, domesticated, as though wood-pigeons were the choristers of some unctuous nonconformist deity. He appreciated this and I reminded him how Cathy in *Wuthering Heights* declared that she could not die because she found that the pillow on which her head rested was stuffed with pigeons' feathers.

'I had forgotten,' he said, 'but I knew that Boswell suffered from insomnia in the Hebrides because his bolster stank of the decayed plumage of sea-fowl and that Dr. Johnson at breakfast called him a fool, saying that, for himself, he would as lief lay his head upon a bag of guillemot feathers as those from a hen-wife's cabin.' I was amused by this sally.

A very odd thought now darted into my mind. I knew that the Pixley family ' deduced its lineage ' from a seal which some time in the Middle Ages had come sliding over the sea-banks of the west of Ireland to lodge with a King's daughter, and as I watched Randal talking to me on the familiar terrace that smelt so sweetly strong of syringa and blown June roses I could not but fancy the legend to be a true one, so unlikely did the young man look, and so soft and dreamy and blameless did his brown eyes appear, as near as may be to those set by nature in the slippery round skull of the great Silkie of Sule Skerrie.

I am a man, upo' the lan',
An' I am a silkie in the sea ;
And when I'm far and far frae lan'
My dwelling is in Sule Skerrie.

There had been a few moments' silence. Pixley poked at the gravel with his walking-stick and I kept wondering to myself what kind of feathers I would collect for Dittany's pillow if I were to be commissioned for such a labour. The breast feathers of innumerable willow-wrens, perhaps, only it would take me a life-time and longer to gather enough of them together, for I knew she would insist that they must all be taken from birds that had died natural deaths. If ever I accomplished my task, I felt sure she would have wonderful dreams, her white cheek resting upon her white hand and her hand upon the white linen that enclosed hundreds of dainty yellow-green feathers plucked from those soft bosoms.

At last the silence was broken. 'I came to tell you,' he began, 'that I have met your mediæval young lady. I ventured to go to her house yesterday morning and persuaded her to come with me to Glastonbury.'

And she had said she could not meet me for four days ! A dull sense of impending destitution descended upon me as with my eyes fixed upon a leaning apple-tree where the redstart had nested that year, I listened. Love and Lordship like no fellowship. I had not been pleased when Dittany had mentioned Randal Pixley's name on Hunger Hill, but the knowledge that they had now met and that he had already taken such unexpected advantage filled me with a heavy foreboding.

And this is Dictam which we prize,
Shot shafts and darts expelling !

185

I do not think I betrayed any emotion. If Randal Pixley had realized in those early days how much I loved her, perhaps everything would have been different. He had come, I think, to see me on that afternoon because of a vague unease about his impulsive trespassing, and I have little doubt he was relieved by my apparent indifference. But I had not forgotten the proverb of the Swiss peasantry, 'It is easier to over-watch a bag of fleas than a pretty maid,' nor that of the Arabs either, their wits nourished with camel's milk, 'If you put butter in the sun it will melt,' or, in truth, that of our homely Dorset folk, 'Free with her lips, free with her hips.'

He told me of their day's excursion. 'She is an exceptional girl,' he kept repeating. 'I don't think I've ever known a more charming companion. I found that she was better informed about the lore of Glastonbury than I am. She knew that Arviragus, the British chieftain, who conducted Joseph of Arimathea to Glastonbury, was a cousin of Caractacus, and that Caractacus himself is buried under the barrow on Hamboro Tout, near Lulworth. She climbed with me to the top of the Tor and we saw that old carving of the woman milking and later we visited the Chalice Well.' I could stand it no longer. 'Glastonbury,' I interrupted rudely, 'is well called " glassy island." Nothing but a succession of mirage-fantasies has been mirrored from its deceitful acres for two thousand

186

years. I have moods when all those superstitious Glastonbury traditions seem pernicious nonsense exactly suitable
to the mentality of the high church clergy and their silly
well-to-do women adorers. Glastonbury breeds lies as
a sow's back breeds lice. We all know that Joseph of
Arimathea never really set foot in England. We all know
that his famous thorn never really blossomed in the winter.
We all know that St. Patrick was never buried at Glastonbury and that the coffin Henry the Second dug up, was
put there by monkish swindlers and never was King
Arthur's ; just as nowadays we all know that Jesus never
rose from the dead !' I leaned back a little ashamed,
but Randal Pixley seemed only entertained at my out-
burst. Spontaneous expressions of feeling invariably
pleased him, and the more outrageous I became the more
urbane and confidant was he. My conversation that afternoon was not exactly polite, but, for all that, as I walked
with him across the lawn, I still felt appreciation of his
personality, although my talk had no doubt been
prompted by the resentment that it was he and not I
who had first shown Glastonbury to Dittany. How I
would have loved to have seen her drink at the leg-
endary fountain whose waters have never ceased to
flow up to the green surface of the ancient garth century
after century. Deeply I envied him. Dittany at Glastonbury must have been the prettiest sight, as full of grace

as a hare drinking out of a green downland pond. I knew so well how she would appreciate every implication of what she was doing and yet would remain essentially untouched, sceptical always and always romantic. Her beauty was not of the kind that is easily given to God. She was like a child who swings herself higher and ever higher among apple-tree blossoms, happy in the green silence broken only by the swish of petticoats, and with no will to reach to the far heavens. Dittany might conceivably give her red gold, her station, her mind, to God, but not the beauty of her body, not her carnal beauty though the water of the freshet were never so fair.

Beauty-in-the-ghost, deliver it, early now, long before death
Give beauty back, beauty, beauty, beauty back to God, beauty's
    self and beauty's giver.

Such words might come from the pilled priest in the conspiring dusk till his eunuch's voice was trebly cracked, but she would remain always loyal to the older, sweeter fealty, and with loveliest lips laughing lightly would pass out through the cloister postern free and unbeguiled on to the summer road of dust and dandelions and traveller's joy !
    When Pixley had gone my mind was even more troubled and I set out for a walk. Truly the old books had been right to describe the root of the herb dittany as they had

done. 'If a man should smell to this wort—behold ! its
naked roots savour of a lemon's rind and are to mortal
lips more acerb and sourish than aloes or the coloquintida.'
'Self-harming jealousy !—fie, beat it hence ! ' I walked by
the side of the mill-stream and then to a solitary Scotch fir
that stood, and still stands, in the middle of the field overlooking the mill-stream water. I sat down at the foot
of this strong signal tree, ruddy as Esau, trying to win
serenity of spirit. It had been a favourite spot of mine
ever since, on a frosty night, I had come here, leaving the
quiet Christmas-holiday schoolroom with my brother
Willie working away at his rabbit nets, and with Bertie
bending over his drawing-board under the lamp, to
undergo an experience that had influenced the direction
of my whole life, deeply fixing the memory of this tree
in my mind as a kind of outward sign-post of an
intellectual turning. The fields over which I had come
that night had been stiff with hoar frost, each leaf of grass
glittering more miraculously than the stars above, and the
more open spaces of the meadows scintillating about me
in all directions like unending seas of frozen quick-silver.
Tingling under the inspiration of so unusual a sight I had
found myself standing beneath this Scotch fir in a mood
of exultation. Scarcely aware of what I was doing I had
thrown my arms about its red rough tangible girth and
with my young eyes fixed upon the moon had striven

to awake myself for ever out of the ' dull soul swoon ' of common day, awake myself to an alert and lively apprehension of the accident of finding myself a free and cognizant being upon so conjured a planet. It had not been to him who died ' on the tree ' that I had called but rather to him who lives ' in the tree,' as I stood alone in the tremulous eagerness of youth in this cold gleaming corner of the astral cosmos.

The tree, alas ! that summer evening could not establish me a second time. I looked at the mill-stream and remained unmoved. I looked at the burdock spinney and it soothed me not at all. One beats the bush and another catches the bird. I could not lift my mind out of the evil drop-trap into which it had fallen. At the bottom of my belly I found my fury. What right had he to take Dittany to such a place, ' deep meadow'd, happy, fair with orchard lawns ' ? I rose presently and kept on towards Lufton, while ever and ever across the darker places of my mind jealousy slowly dragged ' the scaly Horrour of his foulded tail.' I well recollect as I approached the sheep washing-pool on the other side of the railway embankment near the stone bridge how I found relief in petulantly kicking up the dry cow-pats which, round as pancakes, were scattered about in the field. It seemed to give me a peculiar satisfaction to cause these quoits of dung to roll out of my path. My violent pastime exposed discs of albino-pale grasses with beetles and centipedes and such-like fry all confounded to a panic-scramble by the sudden removal of their sheltering canopy. Gradually the quiet of those Lufton footpath ways, ' unspeakable rural solitudes,' brought me back to better sense. As the fool thinks, so the bell chinks. What had really happened ? nothing ! I was like the Langport eel crying out before I was skinned. Why should not Dittany go to Glastonbury with this young man ? It did not necessarily mean that she would forsake me for him, forget our love in an hour with all our kisses sealed in vain :

> *You'll ne'er get kiss o' her comely mouth*
> *Tho' you sh'uld break your heart.*

I muttered the words incautiously, maliciously. In any case why should I now for so little make myself swallow ' poisons more deadly than a mad dog's tooth ' ?

21

Bright are the oak tops,
Bitter are the ash tips,
Sweet the hedge shelter,
Loud the waves roar,
The face cannot hide off
The heart's painful sore.

LLYWARCH HÊN

I WAS TO MEET DITTANY BY THE GREAT BEECH TREE ON Saturday at eleven o'clock. On the Friday I spent the morning looking for some hidden place where we could make love the next day without any chance of being disturbed. Eventually I found what I wanted in a forest of high bracken above the Beeches. I should think I must have taken fully an hour preparing our bed. It was a perfect place. At one end of where I had trampled was a sapling ash and I cut deeply into its bark the words, ' She heard the bridles ring.' It was a line from a ballad describing the girl alone and on a moor at midnight waiting for her lover to ride by with the Fairy Court. The cutting of the five words took me a considerable time. When I had finished I remained in the ferny bower. I could not believe that perhaps in twenty-four hours I should have Dittany in this privy place alone ; the mere thought of such a possibility made me languish. I resolved to mark her footprints secretly as she walked to it and the next day to dig up one or two of the privileged white trefoil clods, and put them in pots and place the pots on the window-sill of the nursery for the growing of some flower or myrtle slip—to keep me in close memory of her through the wintry months !

What a green lair it was that I had found ! and how lovely and how aphrodisiac in its sylvan rudeness was the smell of the crushed bracken ! Oh ! but how I would love her here ! What sweet employments there would be between us, with what passionate love I would kneel before her, looking down upon her ! For a long time I stayed there, my imagination holding her fast, made wild by the thought of her. What was this life where it was possible to meet such a creature clothed in perishable clay ? How could marrow-filled bones, hollow as oboes, be covered with so paragon a plaster of quickened dust ? If Dittany were quit of her frock I would but love her the more, but if she were quit of her flesh would I love her bare bones ?

You are not proud ; you know your birth :
For your embroider'd garments are from earth.

It is said that when Fair Rosamund died in Henry the

Second's absence he became so distraught with proper grief that nothing would suit him but to have the girl's body dug up from the grave so that he could once more look upon that by which he had been for so many years so passionately bewitched.

> 'For him thought that shee passed al wymen in bewtye . . . And whanne the grave was opened . there sate an orrible tode upon her breste bytwene hir teetys, and a foule adder bigirt hir body about in the middle . . . Than the Kynge dyde shette agen the grave and did wryte :
>
> *Here lyeth in grave Rose of the World, but not clene rose.*
>
> And she stanke so that the kyng, ne non other might stond to see that oryble sight.'

If I came upon Dittany one day like a dead hind in a wintry ditch, the ligaments of her vertebræ gnawed at and frayed by the teeth of rats, of necessity those dainty orts would mean little to me, save the mind-trouble of awakened memories. What did I love then ? Was it only an unenduring image whose essence no man could ever see ? Here in truth was a wayward planet lying bland under the procreant sun, as round, irresponsible, and grinning as a hollowed out All-Hallowe'en turnip

194

lantern ! Beasts with wit running about on two legs, beasts without wit running about on four legs, beasts with chops as hairy as devils' faces pushing through nettle hedges, and all this taking place to the tune of the Kingsbury jig and then nothing left but a spadeful of dusty nine-pins in the key-cold earth. What marvels were to be sighted in every crack and cranny! Pliny declared that he had seen flints with ways worn upon their surface by the industrious footfalls of ants. The sleeveless butterfly world so giddy and elusive, the bird world, the edacious duck-pond world, the fern world with its whispering reserves, what a gazing-stock they were, shifting and transitory, restless and mercurial, full of shadows, and imperceptible movements, and magical transmutations ! Where all is at odds, all at adventure, how is it possible for bevies of haunted spirits, bevies of spirits that can be seen and touched, to go their ways,hot to the heel, with envy, hatred, malice, and blackest jealousy jagging at their hearts ?

Dittany and I had often visited a dell under some great oak trees in Stoke Wood, ' tall oaks, branch-charmed by the earnest stars.' The glade was really part of the earthwork trench which runs from Stoke Wood to Ham Hill. It was not a very safe place for us to play in, but I had often given her a kiss there and the thought now came into my head to walk to it. We had named it Dancing Dell.

I had a mind to pass the time by cutting our initials on a
tree-trunk so as to surprise her with them the next time
we were there. I walked by the side of the wall in a
love-sick mood. I proposed to myself to get over into
the wood just opposite the oak trees, for the fosse ran
along the whole length of it on its woodland side. This
grey wall of Ham stones sun-weathered and rain-
weathered had always been a favourite haunt of butterflies
and my brother Bertie and I used to come here to get
good specimens of gate-keepers.

I reached the place and with my hands resting on a
mossy stone was looking for a good crack in which to
insert the toe of my boot when I fancied I heard a low
murmur of voices. There was living at Stoke at that time
an unkempt little village girl whom I had named the Hamadryad, and she was often to be seen in the woods with a
troop of brothers and sisters, gathering sticks. At first I
supposed that she and her little wretches were in the glade.
I climbed over the wall and as quietly as I could moved
through the brush-wood until I had reached a position
from where I could look into the overshadowed fosse
undetected.

What I saw has been seared into my memory. Dittany
was sitting with her back to me, and Randal Pixley,
resting, debonair as ever, against a fallen tree-trunk, was
smoking a cigarette by her side. Hi ! Hi ! Hi ! the

dainty lovers ! I withdrew as silently as I had come. I might have received a gunshot, a gunshot wound that left me stunned but still able to walk. I was suddenly incapable of all thought, possessed by one desire—to be alone. In the disorder of those moments certain facts obtruded themselves starkly. They must already be lovers and Dittany must have shown him our secret retreat. Christ ! where were ' the gate-keepers ' of our Dancing Dell, and where the trusty warders of Dittany's chastity ? I tried to think, to call reason to my help, but like snake-dragons my very bowels lifted up their heads to hiss. I was walking now faster and faster. ' I am hurt,' I found myself saying, ' I am hurt.' He that talks to himself talks to a fool. ' Where should I go ? What should I do ? ' As I walked I went over everything in my mind. She could not, she could not love me. She could never have really loved me, that was plain and the raw truth. All through the ages beautiful girls had been like that. Good ware need seek no chapman. Of course they were like that. My Ilchester Bridge reflections had been correct. She was in love with being loved and that was all.

Because I am a dark haired may,
A damsel dark, a damsel young,
I was not born to say men nay
And make a many shifts at love.

197

Pixley was rich, well-bred, free, and I myself had noted his physical attraction. My kind of adoration must already be striking her as dull and sentimental. It did not keep her in any kind of doubt. It was heavy, tedious, always the same, the same, the same.

But how could she so easily, so lightly go over to the stranger? I could hardly doubt that he had been more exacting with her on the mossy ground of Stoke Wood than any Sultan of Zanzibar had ever been with the damsel of his choice upon the vert ottoman of his noonday chamber. Without doubt Randal Pixley had kissed and handled her till their lust was one. The fool saith, 'Who would have thought it?' He was well-versed as likely as not in the works of Astyanassa—the scholarly mirror-maiden of Helen of Troy's bower, who, according to Saidas, was the first writer in the world to catalogue possible lascivious postures. They *must* be intimate. Had I or had I not heard him call her 'darling'? In any case he had only to lift his hand and she had come to his finger like my mother's white dove, like one of Aphrodite's hen sparrows fluttering, twittering invitations from crest to crutch. And in how many days? In how many hours? Better not to think of it. He that's afraid of the wagging of feathers must keep from among wild fowl. The only possible thing to do was to forget her. I would forget her, forget her voice, forget her eyes, forget her white hands, with fingers slender and small. I would strangle my love for her, as I might pull off the head of a young partridge—a bird rumoured, I remembered bitterly, to be addicted to the most luxurious extravagances if ever it lost its mate. I had been happy before I met her and what was to prevent my being happy again ? Give me my poor quiet life with my homely but comfortable grey pease. But though I could think these brave thoughts my emotions were all up in riot.

I got over the wall into Dogtrap near where the Roman Villa was excavated. For the first time in my life I was under the lash of the cat-o'-nine-tails of jealousy, and I nearly jumped out of my skin for the pain I felt :

> *He kissith hir, and clippith hir ful ofte,*
> *And on hir wombe he strokith hir ful softe.*

How far had Randal Pixley gone in these few hours ? I had woo'd Dittany for days, for weeks, before we had made our green cabinet under the leaves of Norton Covert.

> *Ay, and by heaven, one that will do the deed*
> *Though Argus were her eunuch and her guard.*

In that one glimpse I had had of her between an oak and a green holly I had seen that she was examining her elbow stained by grass and mould—*She had been lying on her back !* —I was now passing in my flight the copse of young beeches that hid the wishing-stone. The image of her, the mere thought of her standing so statue-like on the cushioning moss and polypody ferns under the light leaves, her knees, her elbows, her girlish buttocks so cool beneath her dress of weft linen, galled me to the quick. How happy we had been that day ! Damn him to hell ! he had looked so graceful and confident smoking his cigarette ! As soon as ever he saw her, the great Silkie must have laid her flat ; in half an hour, in a less time even.

> *I thought her*
> *As chaste as unsunn'd snow. O, all the devils !*
> *This yellow Iachimo, in an hour,—was't not?—*
> *Or less,—at first?—perchance he spoke not, but*
> *Like a full-acorn'd boar, a German one,*
> *Cried ' O ! ' and mounted.*

How fraught these words are with the frenzied imaginings of the poet who wrote them, at the vision perhaps of *his* light lady wrapping a stableman's coat about her drooping shoulders, wrapping it about them with the same fingers that he had so often watched pluck at the strings of a lute :

> *How oft, when thou, my music, music play'st—*

fingers used now, alack, in preparations for her disguised departure from the palace yard. With velvet tread she would tiptoe across the moon-blanched cobbles, stealthily, from gable shadow to gable shadow, until with her dark eyes shining, cheeks aflame, and a stifled cry, she could throw herself exposed and shameless, nothing withheld, into the calculating arms of her selfish lover hotly eager for her riggish passion.

22

Here may ye see that women be
In love, meek, kind, and stable ;
Let never man reprove them than,
Or call them variable.

BALLAD

HOW OFTEN HAVE PEOPLE SAID TO ME, ' YOU MAKE too much of sex. It does not play so important a part in life as you imagine.' Let no one give a moment's attention to such opinions. The mere holding of them means that the finer, deeper values have been sacrificed to the coarser, shallower values of society, to public opinion, to considerations of respectability, and to worldly success. Sex is the pulse-beat of life. It is the root, the straight long cow-parsley root that reaches down to the antipodes and which even the dwarfs cannot pull up !

Just so may love, although 'tis understood
The mere commingling of passionate breath,
Produce more than our searching witnesseth :
What I know not : but who, of men, can tell
That flowers would bloom, or that green fruit would swell

To melting pulp, that fish would have bright mail,
The earth its dower of river, wood, and vale,
The meadows runnels, runnels pebble-stones,
The seed its harvest, or the lute its tones,
Tones ravishment, or ravishment its sweet,
If human souls did never kiss and greet?

I remember as a very little boy being taken to a children's party in a neighbouring country house. It was still light when we got into the carriage hired from the Fleur-de-Lis at Stoke, but it soon grew dark, so that, looking out of the windows, I could only make out the moving lights from the carriage-lamps falling upon water in the road puddles, or illuminating for a moment cold wintry banks under a bare hedge. My father used to refer to the carriage a little contemptuously as ' Chant's conveyance,' but I, as a child, never got into it without a feeling of romantic excitement, a feeling which I think had its origin in my memory of one particular party. The ceiling of ' Chant's conveyance ' above the upholstered cushions was covered with a kind of wallpaper such as is often to be seen pasted in the inside of old-world travelling trunks. It impressed my imagination that we could be carried along these unknown country roads in such a domesticated room with only the clop-clop of a horse's feet to remind us that we were abroad. When we reached our destina-

tion on the evening of that party, we were entertained
with a magnificent Christmas-tree. I made friends with
a little girl in white, collecting for her all the coloured
tapes, ribbons, and string that I could pick up amongst
the festive litter left on the floor from the parcels that
had been opened. Presently we were taken to a large
hall, and to my astonishment my little friend in her white
frock went up alone on to a prepared stage and began
to dance what was known in those days as 'the skirt
dance.'

> *Little lad, little lad*
> *Where was you born?*
> *Far off in Somerset under a thorn*
> *Where they sup honey milk from out a ram's horn.*

I was absolutely spell-bound. She danced like a dapper
elf, now poising herself on one tiny toe and now on the
other, now throwing her little legs high into the air ;
she whirled about like a flower caught in a devil's dust-
storm. I had never seen anything so exciting in my life.
I did not know such wonders were allowable. Indeed
I have always considered that it was this little girl's daring
performance which first initiated me into what is after all
by far the most precious entrancement of life. Sitting
there in my velvet knickerbockers it was as if I had been
suddenly transformed by sorcery into a flame of pure fire

so taut did my attention become, far beyond anything experienced by me before in the innocent sequence of my childhood days of hoops, jabberwock hide-and-seek, and bible-reading at my mother's knees.

No settled senses of the world can match the pleasure of that madness.

★   ★

After I had seen Dittany and Randal Pixley together in the dell I found it difficult to sleep. All night long it rained and I kept waking. I lay listening to the drops of rain as they fell, and to the ' clamours through the wild air flying.' My distraught mind envied the patience of the rooted vegetation. I felt afraid of my love for her ; thought of it now with dread and now with an agony of anxiety.

The next morning I was waiting at the beech tree as we had planned. It was a silver Saturday. Would she come ? Years and years seemed to have gone by since our day on the Ilchester river. Seeing what I had seen had increased rather than diminished my passion. The worse I fared the more I loved her. Love creepeth where it cannot go. I never could show pride with Dittany. I knew I would always be willing to accept the slights and flouts of a year to be with her for an hour.

Thistles are a salad for an ass. I would be willing to suffer any humiliation submissively if only God and man would allow me still to *see* her.

Well, I will love, write, sigh, pray, see, groan :
Some men must love my lady and some Joan.

After the wet night Stoke Wood was sparkling, tingling with raindrops, every dangling leaf gave out a bright light. If only I could have been happy, as the dew hangs i' the wood, gay lady ! It was the very background for her after such a mackerel gale. The trees of Stoke Wood had always seemed to me to be confederate with our meetings ; bystanding witnesses, dumb and strong, of the ways of lovers. I had had a letter from my brother John, and he had written of trees in America whose span of life had outstretched the whole history of Christianity, trees that were vigorous already with centuries of growth on the afternoon of the crucifixion, on the afternoon when Mary Magdalene's eyes had been blinded with tears for the only man she had ever loved and the only man who had not so much as offered to caress her white suppliant body.

Suddenly I caught sight of Dittany in the distance. My long-suffering resolutions vanished as soon as I saw her. Before she had reached the great Hedgecock gate she knew that something was the matter. It is soon espied where the thorn pricketh, and well wots the cat whose beard she licketh. She must have had her meetings with Randal on her mind all the time. When we came to the wide trackway where the pink campions grew I stood still. She is pretending, I thought indignantly, that she does not know what the trouble is.

'It is,' I said, 'because you have been meeting Randal Pixley. The very first young man who appears you allow to make love to you. Are you mad, Dittany, to be won with a feather and lost with a straw? We have only to be separated for a few hours and all our happiness is forgotten, and although you told me you could not leave your mother for four days, you let yourself be taken by a perfect stranger to Glastonbury.'

For the first time I saw a flash of anger in Dittany's eyes. She ignored Glastonbury. 'I don't love him,' she answered obstinately. 'I only love you.' I was not reassured. But I was wise enough to take the mutinous flash as a warning. Soft words break no bones. I loved her far too deeply and was far too uncertain of her not to wish to avoid a real quarrel. I became cautious, on my guard, determined at all costs not to estrange her. The words 'I only love you' had been uttered, I knew, under constraint. 'I like Randal Pixley,' she said, 'but I do not like him in that way, and in any case he is a properly brought up young man who would never go any further than holding hands.' She gave me now a tentative look, as much as to say, 'Don't let us spoil our time together. Do let us be friends now.'

She was wearing that morning her soft grey over-coat because of the doubtful weather, and she stood before me white as flowers with her two hands clasped. I would not be placated. 'Dittany,' I said reproachfully, 'how could you, how could you take him to our Dancing Dell, a place we found together and where we have been so happy? Couldn't you choose some other retreat for holding hands?' I could see she was taken aback. She could manœuvre, misrepresent, deceive, lie with felicity and composure, as long as she was sure there was no chance of being discovered. I did not know what had happened there, but I saw that the mere mention of the Dancing Dell had taken her completely by surprise. She looked utterly bewildered. Deceit, weeping, spinning, God hath given to women kindly, while they may live. To gain time she began, like any twitter-light lady, to cry. I had never seen her in tears before and could hold out no longer. We sank down together on the grass by the deep cart-ruts and I did my best to comfort her. She threw her arms about me. 'I do, I do love you so,' she cried. Her cheeks were as wet as the grass we were lying on. She remained quite still with her eyelids closed.

For if we do but chance to bow,
They'll use us then they care not how—
Balow, la-low!

Two emotions were following each other in me. One was a purely æsthetic emotion of wonder at her beauty, her fair face so chaste, each eyelash so fresh, and as symmetrical as the hairs that ridge the edges of new beech-leaves. The other prevailing emotion was one of un-regenerate lust. I longed to possess utterly and utterly this lovely creature pale-washed by all the rains of the heavens. I longed to ravish her with ruthless violence till she should cry her heart out, prostrate and undefended there on the purple water-mint. This lawless impulse to seize upon her there and then, and to subject her, humiliating her utterly *while she was crying,* for a moment possessed me quite. It ran like fire through my body. I wanted to serve her in such a way that she would never, could never forget it, but would be drowned and drowned in tears. Then my eyes fell upon her handkerchief, clenched tight in her hand, hardly big enough for the holding of a Spanish chestnut or meadow mushroom, and at once these reprobate instincts were at an end. I knew in a flash that I would always as long as I lived do anything to relieve her of the lightest trouble, let her go free, be anything, do anything if only she could be happy.

For all that this morning had begun so sadly I still cherish its memory. The bracken bed I had prepared made a perfect couch for love-making. Alone with her again in so secret a place I forgot everything. Lying side by side under a summer sky mottled and dappled as a trout's belly, we looked into the green miniature glens of the bracken forest illumined by splashes of sunshine. Because of the late maiden showers we lay on her grey overcoat and on my overcoat and from these wool-dry islands spied at a new diminutive world glimmering and wet.

We saw a grasshopper, with physiognomy more terrible than that of a pterodactyl, balanced on a stalk ; and upon an outspread frond a skipjack-beetle loitered complacently sunning itself. 'I will give you a gold ring,' she whispered, ' " a ring of troth," and on it I will have engraved the words that were found on the inner rim of the bridal ring that they dug up the other day at Cart Gate—*MY CHOYSE*. When you look at it you will never as long as you live doubt again my true love.'

It was extraordinary how, when we were together, some imaginative affinity, some native physical susceptibility, made it possible for us to step clean out of time and enter freely into some new world of our own where romance was instant in the very grass leaves, in the very mud that received the pressures of her heels. Again I persuaded her to unloose her hair. How living it smelt, like handfuls of pine needles warm in the sun ! So must Iseult's hair have smelt as she held Tristram in her arms protected from the weather by cold castle walls. How Christians manage to reconcile themselves to their irksome abnegations I cannot imagine ! An ass is cold even in the summer solstice ! I would always have put my soul in jeopardy for a snatched hour with this girl.

It was Dittany's idea that morning for us to play at being Aucassin and Nicolette. I was to leave her in her arbour asleep, lulled to sleep by drowsy syrups, and then to come looking for her. I was to find her sleeping. While I was waiting to return to her I thought about the old story : how Nicolette applied the juice of celandines to her body to take away the dark stains of her minstrel disguise before presenting herself at the Castle of Beaucaire. Under the young fir trees at the top of the beeches I gathered a handful of bluebells, ' the honour of the field.' I had always delighted in these wild hyacinths which by the end of the month of May would startle the sight with their pools of blue beneath the beech trees of Park Covert. I loved these hanging bells, these rain-washed blue bells, I loved the juice in their stalks, the very seminal sap, pearly and glutinous, of the rougher woodland gods ! Bluebell juice ! I would anoint her ivory white body with it in the place of the celandine balsam of the poem. ' Your baths shall be the juice of July flowers.' I gathered a handful of foxgloves also. How lovely the long spotted trumpets were with their hairy throats hanging down in shadow ! How exquisite is each morsel of Nature's handiwork, from the blotched patches on a leopard's jacket to the coloured freckles of one of these flowers ! A bumble bee appeared, girdled with gold as for a banquet, and with buzzing preoccupation explored one of the satin-soft, dangling orifices of the flowers in my hand, pressing its body, humming like a gong, ever further and further into the mottled floral cavern. Afraid lest it should presently sting Dittany with its thrusting scimitar I brushed it away and saw it disappear over the tops of the spreading ferns in its tireless quest for fresh festivals.

I returned through the bracken. Dittany was lying with her cheek resting on her hand. ' Her breath is her own which scents all the year long of June, like a new made haycock.' I had often persuaded her to breathe into my mouth, so that her spirit, her life might become one with mine ; but now I could see no indication that she breathed or even lived. She was always good at pretending. She lay still.

> *Like unto Maia, when as Jove her took*
> *In Tempe, lying on the flowry gras,*
> *Twixt sleepe and wake, after she weary was.*

I waited for a little before waking her. She had arranged her frock—with what ' wild civility ' !—and her cheeks were flushed.

> *Right cheek ! Left cheek ! Why do ye burn ?*
> *Cursed be she that doeth me harm !*
> *If she be maid, let her be slayed ;*
> *If she be widow let her mourn ;*
> *But if my own true love—burn, cheek, burn !*

And still, and still she pretended to sleep, and I would never have known she wasn't sleeping if I had not seen that her lips were just perceptibly curled in a strange way as if she herself were abandoning herself to an utter indulgence of hot girlish dreams.

> *On the flowering bed*
> *When the sun was high*
> *You kissed my breast*
> *And you kissed my thigh.*
> *Your body then*
> *Was a sword to mine,*
> *Our mouths together*
> *Were drinking wine.*

How we drowned each other in our love, she fetching her breath ' as short as a new ta'en sparrow ' and I out of all measure luxurious. I have often imagined the enchant-

ment that Odysseus must have felt when in the moonlit
cave he would hold the naked body of Calypso in his
strong mariner's arms. How sweet she always was to
him, even at the end carrying augers to him over the
flowery hayfields for the building of his raft in the pine
forest ! Did the shadowed cowrie secret of her nymph's
body, willing Lady as she was, drive him frantic with
its evasive seaweed smell ? And when the stiff mediæval
gown dropped from Iseult's hips did Tristram fall upon
his knees before the proud enchanted panther-black
triangle knowing for certain that nothing else mattered
in life ?

> *With great delight*
> *Flaunting her loveliness,*
> *How it became her well !*

We had to leave our happy bed at last. As we climbed
through the ferns and young sapling trees I looked back.
Already the green ' form ' where we had been wore an
aspect desolate, deserted, indifferent. By the autumn
there would be left no registering shoe-mark of our
summer joy amongst the rusty dying bracken.

> *The flowers and thymy air,*
> *Will they now miss our coming ?*
> *The dumbles thin their humming*
> *To find we haunt not there ?*

LOVE AND DEATH

We now walked across the fields to the group of Scotch firs above Stoke Wood. I was tormented by the thought of ever having to leave her even for a moment. What would I not give to live those past sweet moments over and over again, for ever and ever, world without end ! They had been chances of a deep and ultimate rapture and I knew it. Whenever in my after-life I heard people say that it was impossible to be really happy in this world, I knew that they lied. That hour and a half in the bracken was an hour and a half of a sunshine happiness as actual and as positive as a field of daisies. What monstrous mendacity to say that the gratification of the sexual appetite is not by far the supreme solace of human life. Worldly-minded people, occupied with pomps and vanities, must most surely execrate this benison solely for the purpose of gammoning the young.

We came up to the Scotch firs and I began asking her when we could next meet. I anticipated enjoying a long blackberry-summer with her. Looking round with a nervous sideways glance she said, ' Llewelyn, I meant to have told you, we are going away to Italy next Saturday. Mother is no better and the doctor thinks she should leave England at once.'

The shock of this announcement threw me utterly down. I felt benumbed, amort, knowing only that a new calamity had, when it had been least expected, fallen upon my

215

head ; then slowly I came to my senses, outraged beyond reason that she could have kept such vital information from me.

'Never mind, Llewelyn,' she said, putting her hand lightly upon my wrist. 'Never mind, I shall be back again ; and we will play together again. I shall always love you whatever happens.'

'But how do I know you will always love me?' I answered fiercely. 'It is a matter about which I can feel little confidence. You go to Glastonbury with your new love, and then you lead him tickle-footed to our Dancing Dell !'

I remember she made no answer, but standing with her back against the red trunk of a Scotch fir she looked at me silently as though my reproaches stirred in her nothing but pity. This girl of eighteen years looked at me with compassionate eyes and her grave gaze of solicitude disturbed me.

'I don't believe you have ever loved me, Dittany, not really loved me,' I muttered, and, against my very pride, a strong wave of self-commiseration swept over me. I felt the skin of my face growing stiff and my features beginning to pucker and I turned my head away, though not before she had realized how deeply unhappy I was. 'Forgive me, forgive me, Lulu,' she said impetuously, throwing her arms about my neck ; 'you must, you must forgive me. I swear to you by the ferns upon which we have been lying that I do love you, and I shall always love you. Oh ! stop, oh, do stop ! I can't bear it, and listen, listen to me. I will prove to you how truly I love you. I will give myself to you entirely and that will bind us for ever.' Her words made me again hope. I threw my arms about her. ' Listen,' she said, ' I am now sleeping in the summer-house by the fish-pond. On fine nights I drag my cot on to the lawn, but if it rains I stay inside. Come to me after midnight on Thursday. We are leaving on Saturday.'

23

Or what is longer nor the way,
Or what is deeper nor the sea.

. . . . .

O the wind is longer nor the way
And love is deeper nor the sea.

BALLAD

GAIN MY DREAMS AND MEMORIES WERE BROKEN.
I was back on Chaldon Down. Somebody
beckoned to the nurse and presently Gertrude
came to ask me if I would see a clergyman who had
called bringing a present of some hothouse grapes.
A young man in clerical dress now appeared and stood
stolidly in front of my bed. He explained that he had
heard I was ill and felt he would like to come and visit
me. I thanked him. A large red hand emerged from
a white cuff. I felt like Æsop's mouse who, seeing the
cat hanging by her hinder legs from a kitchen peg, holla'd
out, ' Ah, my good friend, are you there ? I would not
trust myself with you though your skin were stuffed with
straw.' Suddenly, without giving warning, he sank down
upon his knees, just as the Arab stallion Ramadan that I
used to ride in Africa would try to do, with me still upon

his back. Pawing the ground with one of his fore-feet he would go down upon his knees as a preliminary to enjoying a roll. I had no *koboko* ready, as in the case of the beast, but I raised my hand in protest and my sister came to my rescue, carrying the clergyman away, before he could utter a word, to have tea with her in her drawing-room. The clerical solecism agitated me. Now I felt indignant, and now I worried lest the young man's feelings might have been hurt. I think I could have tolerated being prayed for by an elderly clergyman, by some venerable old man who would have reminded me of my father, but even such an invasion would have been a trouble to me. He that will not be saved, needs no sermon. The hours of a man's dying are very personal hours and should be scrupulously respected. The spirit should be permitted to draw itself in upon itself, trusting at the last to its own steadfastness. 'I tell thee, fellow, there are none want eyes to direct them the way I am going ; but such as wink, and will not use them.' Without any doubt reliance upon the supernatural is a characteristic of an early stage in the mental development of the human race and is destined clean to disappear. Why we should still have such a breeze in our breech is more than I know. We disbelieve now in wizards, and witches, and warlocks, and later we will disbelieve in Christ ' in the clowdes of heaven with his Taratantara sounding.'

Men and women should accept their earth inheritance unintimidated by the mumbling of clerks greedy for spiritual powers who ' turn their halcyon beaks with every gale and vary of their masters.' It is our own affair to set right the misery of this world and not the affair of imaginary gods. He that pryeth into the clouds may be struck with a thunder-bolt. It is our own affair to see that there is bread for all, and wine for all, and girls for all. Yet mark the craft and energy that have been expended generation after generation in attempts to justify a creed as sickly and savage as Christianity, a creed which can be shown to be nothing but a prodigious falsehood by five minutes' honest thought. Man's best candle is his under-standing. In the Fossil Forest eastward of Lulworth there are ossified Cycadean stools that belong to the Jurassic Age, eight million years ago ; and yet these theological fancy-men are diligent to persuade us, for safety's sake, that an ignorant rumour starting up like a Jack-hare but two thousand years since, contains the solution of our earth's secret, nay, the secret of the whole wide turbulent universe of void and flame. ' Tommy-True-Tongue tell me no tales, nor merry lies. I never loved them.'

Fugitive man, praying to-day and ploughing to-morrow, yearns to believe that his hungry concerns are under the care of a divine Father, which they most certainly are not ;

he yearns to think that the human soul is immortal, which it most certainly is not ; he yearns to believe that Jesus rose from the dead, which he most certainly did not. So it comes to pass that these Abraham-men with thumbs of gold have so large a scope and can swell with high stomachs to such great matters, that at length they have a mind to be arch with our kings, proclaiming scuttlings back to God, to a God as like to themselves as one stockfish to another, with the same limitations, the same lacks of understanding, the same untrustworthy manner of thought—no difference whatever, open which barrel you will, no one the better herring, all salted and all shotten. They have need of a blessing who kneel to a thistle.

> *O God, although through fear I hardly dare*
> *To hint it, all trouble springs from thee.*
> *Hast Thou no sand or gravel in Thy sandals?*

Still, still to this very day do these black-coated Magi play blindman's buff with us, reaffirming their fables with words, words, words ; words like dice, loaded with double sixes at both ends lest their sorceries should miscarry, those profitable sorceries that for two thousand years, day after day, have turned their kitchen spits and caused larded dumplings to bob up and down in well-tinkered ecclesiastical fire-hob pots. ' They give of their

221

goods not a goose's wing.' It is scarcely possible for a bishop to be a good man ; doubt it not, for all their smooth coo-me-doo voices, they are ever dangling after preferments. Believe well and have well. Better gold than God. The Apostolic succession is a succession through two millenniums of the greatest coney-catchers in Christendom. That's never good that begins in God's name. When have any of these proud prelates done a service for the honourable hedge-stick parson who without pelf or pride knows the poor of his village better than baker's pennies—those oppressed poor who for their cursed belly's sake must needs sweat the very skin from off their bones ?

> *Wyd was his parish, and houses far asonder,*
> *But yet he lafte not for reyne or thonder,*
> *In siknesse and in meschief to visíte*
> *The ferthest in his parisshe, smal and great*
> *Uppon his feet, and in his hand a staf.*

The ruling clergy have done us incalculable mischiefs with their fears, their superstitious obsessions, and recreant dreads of life. He that followeth nature goeth not far out of the way. The identification of sexual desire with sin is not only the most morbid and deleterious conception ever invented by our self-torturing brains, but it is also a shocking blasphemy against the procreant urge that quickens the whole of our planetary existence. Even the Jews from whom these prating prelates derive the fads of their faith knew better. The Patriarchs of the Old Testament were never once shamed to lie down with their women-folk upon broad beds of ox-hide tight stretched across olive-wood beams ; and Jesus himself, on the few occasions when he gave his attention to such matters, dismissed them with a reserved utterance of magnanimous ambiguity. How then does it come about that the peevish doctrines prevalent at the present time in the organized churches jump so ill with the humane and natural attitude towards love-pleasures to be learned from the Scriptures ? Is it not the jostling of old forest taboos with the personal morbidities of Paul of Tarsus that provided a teaching as barratrous as is to be found in the Ninth Article of our Prayer Book ?

' Man is far gone from original righteousness, and is of his own nature inclined to evil, so that the flesh lusteth always contrary to the Spirit ; and therefore in every person born into this world, it deserveth God's wrath and damnation.'

The best fish swim near the bottom. The boughs that bear most hang lowest. We have allowed these men to play the jack with our lives long enough. They would make any child abject for the rest of its life.

I wander thro' each charter'd street
Near where the charter'd Thames does flow,
And mark in every face I meet
Marks of weakness, marks of woe.

In every cry of every man,
In every infant's cry of fear,
In every voice, in every ban,
The mind-forg'd manacles I hear.

Is it to be wondered at that so many of us cut our throats or are clapped into Bedlam or worse? How can we hope to live in anything but sorrowful sort when the richest guerdon that life has to offer is hourly being decried, and the free direction of our emotional lives being daily interfered with by a thousand petty pressures? Tacitus marvelled at the high value the Germans placed upon chastity, and without doubt England still suffers from the same unclassical preoccupation.

Birds of a feather flock together,
And so do pigs and swine
Rats and mice will have their choice
And so shall I have mine.

There can be no greater travesty against life than complacently to accept love as a mere pledge of domestic devotion equally devoid of spiritual ecstasy as of the

ravishment of the senses. It is a notable fact that in
Greek mythology, if we except the Furies, the chastity of
Artemis and of Pallas Athene were alone unimpeachable.
' Chastity without charity lies chained in hell. It is but
an unlighted lamp.'

Truth may be blamed, but shall never be shamed. If I
could I would have every boy and girl in England hear
these true words : *Sensuality is the measure of a man's virtue.*

Of course the more mettlesome of our young people
read pornography, scribble obscenities in privies, drink,
riot, and range, and are daily plagued by disillusionment,
seeing that the proper flourishing of their lives has been
for so long a time subordinated to the domicile interests
and mercenary apprehensions of a set of fearful old men,
of a set of foolish old men white of poll and of heart,
who, with obstinate preconceptions, have for century
after century been attempting to exact from the individual
far greater sacrifices than any social contract, however
stiff, has a right to exact.

> *Young blood doth not obey an old decree :*
> *We cannot cross the cause why we were born.*

All restraints upon love-making that are not essential
to the prosperity of the commonwealth are wicked.
Consciously or unconsciously they are directed against
the most natural and most lasting source of human cheer.

Libbety, libbety, libbety-lat,
Who can do this? and who can do that?
And who can do anything better than that?

It should be universally recognized that every boy who opens the womb with love is blessed ; and that every maid who allures a lad by her modern graces to the enrichment of their two lives is serving loyalties far more ancient and far more honourable than those claimed on Sundays for the invisible God of commonalty comfort.

Again and again I have had occasion in my life-time to observe that it is not the professing Christians but the men and women whose deepest life-loyalty is to the senses who concern themselves most about the conditions of tormented human beings, and, indeed, who most effectively study to bring relief to the unnecessary sufferings of animals and mortals. The others will busy themselves in the public eye and will be quite unperceptive of the plight of the dust-man or of their own scullery-maid.

The generous actions of those whom the pious so lightly call 'loose-livers,' men and women born without preconceptions either religious or moral, are more in harmony with life's irresponsible waywardness ; they do not have to be cross-fitted to the petty considerations of fixed principles but obey only a native impulse to open cage doors and to release chained dogs. To put an end to

226

unhappiness is their sole preoccupation. For a man or a beast to be suffering is for them, without further questioning, a sufficient excuse for intervention. This attitude of careless, humane benevolence to all problems, public as well as private, is most commonly to be found amongst people who honestly accept existence on its lowest terms and who, for the very reason that their own creature appetites have been richly gratified, are in no mood to favour fanciful inhibitions, still less, conventional cruelties, whether they be covert or open or merely a matter of use and wont. Such free spirits are too much in love with life's natural joys to countenance greedy exploitations or easily to condone the desolations incident to war.

Men for the most part are apt to mischief, and resort to violence when they carry headpieces splitting with ideals and 'do not mind their lusts.' The French possess a fine old proverb which undoubtedly rose from the soil and which, with a shrewd earth wisdom, goes to the very heart of the matter : ' *Bon animal, bon homme* '. Nietzsche also wrote ' *to attack the passions at the root is to attack life at the root. The praxis of the church is inimical to life.*' As also Stendhal : ' *Sans passion il n'y a pas de vertu.*' William Blake comprehended the wickedness of sexual suppressions that coldly sacrifice nature for the advantage of a primitive property sense—twisting and contorting

the psyches of myriads of children in our Western World
to appease the prejudices of custom and the envy of eld :

> *Abstinence sows sand all over*
> *The ruddy flesh and flaming hair,*
> *But desire gratified*
> *Plants fruits of life and beauty there.*

From his cradle hours in fish shape Paumanok Walt
Whitman too recognized the obliquity of these morbid
expostulations.   How untold is the misery that has resulted
from so frenzied an attempt to break the proud spirit of
the unicorn with horsewhip and crooked curb !   In poem
after poem Walt Whitman celebrates a free and natural
acceptance of the agonies and ecstasies of love passion,
of love passion wanton, wayward, and unrestrained.

Singing the true song of the soul fitful at random,
Renascent with grossest Nature or among animals,
Of that, of them and what goes with them my poems informing.

> . . . . . .

(Hark close and still what I now whisper to you,
I love you, O you entirely possess me,
O that you and I escape from the rest and go utterly off, free
> *and lawless,*
Two hawks in the air, two fishes swimming in the sea, not
> *more lawless than we.)*

Desire at all times and in all places is the highest manifestation of life : except in the case of cruelty, rape, and seduction of the immature, it is never deserving of reproof. These impious and intractable men would have us degrade the supreme creative force, life's profoundest mystery. The camel-driver has his projects and the camel has her projects. Relying upon superstitions of the most crude origins, and upon their own unproven sacerdotal sorceries, they would have us abase ourselves down, down upon our knees before a tortured image of misery's invention, rather than, with hearts enduring and compassionate, to worship the wonder of simply being alive.

Make no doubt of it, any love is better than no love at all. Follow the voice of the fox rather than that of the dog ; the first leads to freedom, the second to the chain of the kennel. The most careless gratification of venery, with mutual delight, constitutes an exalted experience. He begins to die who quits his desires. Far better that we listen to the wild flutings of Dionysus, ' that backward glancing, pied-piper of human consciences,' than lend our ears, even for a single moment, to the life-abusing manias of these saucy saints, who, with no Silenus at their elbow to cup their ears, would have us exchange our real joys for a heaven that we all know well enough exists only in the self-indulgent fancies of a craven crew of trivial men and women. Catch not at the shadow and lose the substance. Bread is still bread, wine is still wine, salt is still salt, and women real to the senses beyond all testimony ; and what we have, we don't have to look for. No longer pipe, no longer dance. With good cause then we may follow, magpie on wrist, the triumphant thoroughfares of the mad God and for at least some hours of our brief lives ' fleet the time carelessly, as they did in the golden world.'

By a deliberate effort of my will I now compelled myself to leave off considering these sorrowful confusions so that I might return to my own memories.

> *Juliet leaning*
> *Amid her window-flowers—sighing—weaning*
> *Tenderly her fancy from its maiden snow*
> *Doth more avail than these.*

24

He that killeth an ox it is as if he slew a man.

ISAIAH

SO UNSETTLING TO ME WAS THE ANTICIPATION OF WHAT Dittany had promised that I could think of nothing else but the dear delight of it, and I hardly worried at all about her going abroad. I had five and a half days to wait.

After my mother had read to me I walked, and after tea I again walked, this time as far as Pitt Pond. This pond was in the middle of a dark wood. There was an island in its centre, and one end was deep and the other shallow. It was in the deep-end that the father of my nursemaid drowned himself. A keeper saw him take his cap off his grey head, lay it carefully on the grass, and jump in, a labourer with a rude and uneducated mind and yet with sufficient intemperance of spirit to reject life. The evening light was still shining through the trees. I regretted that the memories I had of the place were without Dittany. How happy I would have been to have had her with me in former winter-times when the pond was warped with ice, black as horn, ice that would bend and give out cracks resonant under the dark trees even to the very boat-house in the farthest corner. How attentive I would have been to bore the heels of her boots with a gimlet for screwing on her skates, how eager to show her the fish of evil hap which, cruising in the night too near the pond's surface, had been caught and frozen fast in the transparent ice as though into the glass of a floor mirror. I would have showed her also the mother-of-pearl in the fresh-water oyster shells I used to find near the boat-house where the mud was stinking and black, shells that used to appear to me as incomparable as gem-devised ear-shaped ornaments of the rarest invention.

I could not rid my mind of Dittany. All my thoughts led to that morning meadow-path. The rareness of her gentle condition, of her poetical, emancipated being, was already an obsession with me. Thoughts about her had begun to make the furrows in my brain that remain still. As though my mind were being ploughed by her with the grass-green horn of the ballad :

And ye maun plough it wi' your blawin' horn
And ye maun sow it wi' pepper corn.

I thought of her as I crossed the field from Park Covert, hoping that in the following April we would come to that place together at the time when the gorse would be in flower and the air would be smelling of Easter moss and of rainy sunshine. As I went down Hollow Lane and walked through the village, I still had only her in my mind and would have continued to think only of her in the Terrace-Walk had not my attention been diverted by an occurrence that utterly ruined for me the peace of the summer evening. Suddenly the air of the garden rang with an awful crying, half-shriek and half-groan, a terrifying expression of a living creature's ultimate desperation. It was a hoarse, shocking, and unnatural crying, the kind of shrill, guttural, agonized bellowing that might have proceeded from the mouth of the centaur Chiron when he felt the arrow of his favourite pupil pierce his hoof to the quick, causing him, the old rowan-tree mountain-lawn schoolmaster, to neigh and neigh for a release from the curse of immortality. The sound continued at intervals for half an hour. It was a cow that, as they used to say in Somerset, had become ' rafti ' on the way to the village slaughterhouse. The driven animal, under a premonition of its fate perhaps, had sunk down in the middle of the road opposite Lawsell. Nothing could persuade her to get up. The drover beat her, he twisted her tail until we could hear the gristle crackle, but he could not budge her. Eventually the butcher was called and under his competent direction the luggage-truck from the station was borrowed to carry her to her death through the barton gates. Of course I was young in those days, and easily taken in by

the appearance of things. There seemed to me nothing
incongruous about my father providing for the family
table a good sirloin of roast beef with horse-radish and
Yorkshire-pudding every Saturday. Always under scru-
tiny morality, right or wrong, melts away into what is
customary or not customary.

Go into the churches at Christmas and listen to the
words spoken, to the wealth of unseemly sentiment that
issues from the mouths of the preachers. What scot or lot
in the wide plan of redemption have oxen, the patient
oxen of the fields who watched the birth of Jesus, stretching their great heads with eyes more liquid than Juno's
to see what was toward ?

> ' *Here's a fine bag of meat,*'
> *Says the master-auctioneer,*
> *As the timid, quivering steer*
> *Starting a couple of feet*
> *At the prod of a drover's stick,*
> *And trotting lightly and quick,*
> *A ticket stuck on his rump,*
> *Enters with a bewildered jump.*

Herded together, horn to tail, in the shambles of each
little township they await their slaughtering in turn. How
much butcher's broom would be required to cleanse those
Augean stables when the Christmas-week work of the

234

thoughtless young men is over and the joints of fresh flesh have been prepared, haunch and brisket, for the cheerful Christmas-card, orange-glowing shop-window displays of that blessed time? The cow, I learnt afterwards, had been bought at South Petherton. It had been pastured in the peaceful fields by the river Parrett, and surely it was no unknowing creature who had that night lifted up her desperate voice of supplication. Thomas Hardy told me that he had once tried to reason with a Dorset labourer who was maltreating a farm-horse and was astonished to receive the truly Catholic answer, ' But, Measter, the girt beastie b'aint no Christian.'

The white cow's desperation drove the thought of Dittany clean out of my mind. It was an experience that I have always regarded as important in the hardening of my philosophy. 'How does God know? Can he judge through the dark cloud? Thick clouds are a covering to him and he sees not : and he walketh in the circuit of the heaven.' To continue to love life after having once heard the reverberation of so ghastly an outcry was the matter I had to solve. To love life in a cancer hospital, on a battlefield, to love it with an impervious and obstinate loyalty—that is the problem for all disenthralled spirits. That evening experience first taught me my strong doctrine. Because joy holds empire over sorrow, reviving against odds at every chance, the movements of nature must be accepted without cavil or subterfuge, we ourselves, however, being scrupulous not to add a single tear, a single groan, to the dread count of the world's woe. We must accept life as it is, the good along with the bad, like a crop of September plums, some eaten by wasps, some not ; and our morality must be that of the gardener who knows that the next year's August will bring to his trees the same knavish outlaws, and yet is content each season to combat the harm they do ; preserving the purple fruit as best he may, radiant in the sun. That white cow—' Howl ! Howl ! Howl ! Howl ! O ! you are men of stones '— moved me like a trumpet-call ; and from that hour I knew that every honourable spirit deserving of liberation must engage himself in an unending battle against the custom cruelties tolerated by the stupidity and obtuseness of men.

25

As I am a lady true of my promise
Thou shalt be a welcome guest.

BALLAD

THE NEXT DAYS WENT SLOWLY. THURSDAY AT LAST
arrived when every minute seemed an hour and
every hour an age. I could not believe that tea-
time would ever come, and, when it did come and Mary at
last was carrying out the cups and saucers and my father's
egg-plate, I could not believe that the evening would ever
go by. The weather was now more settled so that my
father, looking out of the dining-room window at the
Cole's orchard, had constantly sighed and repeated, as it
were in the form of a pious benediction : ' It is certainly
a most beautiful evening.' From where he had been sitting at the end of the table he had been able to see the
light on the great beech trees near the old house, those
beeches behind which in mid-winter the sun would
rise a ball of red, allowing the candles that had been
used for family prayers to be extinguished, and irradiating the feathers of the blue-tits hanging upside down
on the pieces of fat that my father every winter sus-

237

pended from a child's wooden hoop, crossed by two slats, and nailed in their centres to the top of an old broom-handle firmly planted in a frozen flower-bed outside the window. The light of that evening was lovely, lying so flat upon the sun-browned bents, brushing so lightly the tops of the trees that grew along the West Drive.

After tea I went down to the Terrace-Walk and tried to read ; but I was not very successful. Presently I walked in the orchard thinking to find an early fallen green apple. To hold an apple in the hand gives promise of the last favour. I sauntered up through the field where the walnut-tree was, eventually entering the backyard through the gate by the cowhouse. A mood was upon me which I knew of old, a mood wherein I became suddenly aware of time as if it actually were static, as if the swift flaming of the immortal moments had been suddenly arrested in the cold hand of eternity, and I awake to know it. I had experienced this sensation when I was still a very small boy. Bertie and May were walking up and down the drive with Harry Lyon, laughing and talking. They called to me, but instead of joining them I excused myself and began taking in the collapsible garden-chairs that had been left on the lawn. I could not abide their gaiety just then, for as the beetles hummed into the wire-netting near the variegated maple-tree, and the tennis lawn grew damper and damper, I was being initiated into an aware-

ness of our earth existence that stirred me from crown to
heel. I was still a child, but I had become suddenly
possessed by the liveliest realization of birth and death and
the dream nature of the hours that lay before me to spend
as I liked. I was caught up in a mood far more serious
than became my age as I went about folding up the chairs
and gathering together the painted croquet mallets.

> *The shadows in the garden listen*
> *While the flowers weep.*
> *Why does the door swing on its hinges?*
> *The shadows on the roadway listen*
> *While the grasses sleep.*
> *Why does the gate stand open so wide?*
> *Over the hills where the sun went down*
> *The Messengers come.*
> *They stoop. They stumble. Their hair is white.*
> *They are dumb.*

When on that later evening of impatience and anticipation I felt this same mood come upon me, I crossed over
by the cucumber-frame and, pushing my way through the
currant bushes, sat down in hiding in the middle of some
giant horse-radish plants. It was already cockshut time,
but the swallows were still darting in and skimming
out of the stick-house. I knew that very soon the ever-
lasting-sweet-peas under the toolhouse window would

239

be passively receptive to the night visits of innumerable moths, yellow-under-wing moths, puss moths, ' millery, millery dusty poll,' and satin-bodied tiger-moths of gorgeous tapestry. For some moments I deliberately gave myself up to meditations consciously detached from the ordinary face of those tantalized moments, but this was not for long. My restless thoughts soon took a more intimate and voluptuous turn. Memories of Dittany quickened me with desire, until all against my will I began hotly to dwell upon the beguiling graces of her flesh, upon ' the cunning she had to be strange ' ; until my imagination flamed up at the mere memory of the honey-mark upon her neck, and at the recollection of particular glances she had given me, full of softest implications. The yearning for the moment when I should be sharing the joys of love with her again became almost unendurable. How precious, beyond all count, was the shadowy presence of this beautiful girl, astray in the mesh and murmur of an unimaginable material universe without beginning or end ; a universe, now a riot of fiery torrents, and now the encompasser of vast blanks of silence ; a universe measureless and uninvolved, inviolate, and infinite.

26

I am glad as grasse would be of raine
Great joy that I may take.

BALLAD

IT WAS PAST MIDNIGHT WHEN I FOUND MYSELF CROSSING
the lawn by the fish-pond near the stone summer-
house where Dittany slept. I was wearing a flannel
shirt and flannel trousers under an overcoat. I had been
as silent as I possibly could be, opening and shutting the
gate. I was careful to tread on the grass as I followed
the drive lest I should wake the coachman and his wife in
the lodge.

Dittany was not in the summer-house, but I was presently aware of the whiteness of her bed in the rose-garden.
Pale as a snow-drift it stood under the great sycamore.
I went to it. She was fast asleep, her cheek resting on
her hand in a way that seemed as natural to her as it is to
a bird to rest its head under its wing. The light of the
waning moon, newly risen, fell full upon her. It was after
her fashion, I thought, to be found at such a time asleep.
She could never be deeply implicated in anything that

241

had to do with earth life. Her spirit had always something of the changeling about it. But how utterly lovely she looked dreaming in that garden.

Now sleeps the crimson petal, now the white ;
Nor waves the cypress in the palace walk ;
Nor winks the gold fin in the porphyry font :
The firefly wakens : waken thou with me.

I stood in awe. Except for where her hips made a small rising mound, her form was almost indistinguishable under the coverlet. I could but guess at the position of her knees lying one upon the other, her knees and her white ankles.

And still she slept an azure-lidded sleep,
In blanchèd linen, smooth, and lavendered.

I considered how best I might waken her. 'Dittany,' I whispered. 'Dittany.' She opened her eyes without fear.

'It is you,' she said ; 'I thought you were never going to come. I thought you would be here when I came out at ten, and then I was afraid you weren't coming at all.' She rubbed her eyes and raised herself on one elbow. 'Look at the moonlight on the sycamore,' she whispered. I sat on the edge of the bed. The great sycamore over-

shadowed us with the dreaming woods beyond it. Together in silence we listened to the fitful earth-murmur
of the half-mown hayfields and the mossy orchard-lanes.
Never before had I felt myself more poignantly susceptible
to the quality of her being, diaphanous as the old-
fashioned flower called Love-in-the-mist, more evasive
and privy than the aura of her namesake plant, that,
concealed in its cloud of cerulean haze, used to grow so
abundantly on Mount Dicte in Crete, in glens that trembled not only with the excellent freshness of a seaside
valley, but also with every kind of subtile sorcery. I
wanted to slip out of my clothes and into her bed at
once, but dared not. I was impatient with the fever of
youth, was trembling, but yet had enough wit left in
me to wish to enjoy to the full her childish awakening to such a midnight. The mysterious spirit of the
summer lawns and meadows had become for me
incarnate in Dittany. If she really allows me to embrace
her, I thought, I shall be embracing the sacred night
itself.

What was Dittany whispering to herself now? I could
generally catch her lowest murmur. I think she was
feeling nervous and wished to gain time. I was too
excited, or she was too excited. 'You shall have the
sweet delight, Lover, of me.' She had found herself
suddenly wide awake in the secret garden of a mid-

night moon, vulnerable in mind and body as never
before.

I contrived a ruse to beguile her ; I began to shiver.
I knew this would confound her hesitations. ' Llewelyn,
you are cold,' she said, ' you must come into bed, into
my bed at once.' She gave to these words of my wildest
desire an odd little twist of deprecation. Soon, soon I was
with her, this fair feminine creature. Each thread of
the flaxen sheets kept her body's warmth, the warmth and
sweetness of her body. I put my right arm over her
shoulder, longing to possess her without a moment's
delay, longing to brim the charm and enchantment of her
body with splashes of my living seed. Then I felt under
her arm so tender and so long, something furry like a
muff. ' What have you got *here* ? ' I asked in astonishment. ' It's my kitten ;' and she lifted it above the
blankets by the scruff of its neck. The kitten was too
sleepy even to open its eyes, it just hung in the moonlight with its legs dangling. ' Never mind,' she said,
' there shall be room for three in my bed,' and she put
the small drowsy creature back under the bedclothes.

And in the secret darke, that none reproves,
Their pretty stealthes shal worke, and snares shal spread
To filch away sweet snatches of delight,
Conceald through covert night.

244

I did not leave her until the first birds began to
twitter.

> ' *It is not day,*
> *My sweetheart smooth and white ;*
> *Love bid me stay !*
> *The lark has lied.*'

Ah ! how I cursed those intermittent sounds that came
from bush and tree and cold, wet hedge in the dim
dawn. As she was kissing me good-bye, ' ten kisses short
as one, one long as twenty,' I knew that those swift hours
of love would be for ever the most precious hours of my
life. No expression of emotion could have been devised
more perfect, more explicit, between one human animal
and another, between man and woman apt for every
grace, for every indelicacy. To be allowed to do whatever I wished with Dittany, and to hear her rapid
breaths, her gasping cries, as she felt the power of my
passion pass deeper and ever deeper into her relaxed
body !

> *Thus, having swallowed Cupid's golden hook,*
> *The more she strived, the deeper was she strook.*

The propagating process of flowers is not half so
finished as is that of mortal love, the light billing of birds
is nothing so satisfying. The love between mortals

defeats all celebration. How unanticipated this uniting of airy sprites with enlarged belladonna eyes, in attitudes so maddeningly obscene, in attitudes and actions so conspicuously belonging to the earth ;

And when I lie with love in bed,
A strong kind arm beneath my head,
And my flesh quickening with delight
When my love's body enters in,
No need have I a heaven to win.

Then at last when my mere blind demands were gratified I was possessed by a mood of pure adoration and found myself motionless and holding her in my arms in silence through the stillness of the false dawn, utterly at peace both in mind and in body and utterly loving her with the whole passionate strength of my countryman's imagination, with the whole force of my free religious spirit. As long as men and women can so enrapture each other's senses, earth life is in no desperate case. What does it matter that our days are but as a breath ? Such sensual reciprocities redeem all sorrows, all insults, all abuses, all exploitations. Here is a sufficient quittance of the world's woe.

Hold my hair fast, and kiss me through it soon,
Ah God, ah God, that day should be so soon.

It is in the hour of the fulfilment of love between a man and a woman that the reckless affirmations of mutinous life may best be apprehended. It is then that the vain mind of man, confounded utterly by the roarings of desire, lies open at last to instruction from the senses, from those five unparagoned wits that have become in one snatched instant more piercingly sensible of God's true word than ever are the pelts of frogs to a touch from mortal fingers hot as fire. With lips pressed upon lips and with bodies of tragic flesh fast clinging, the Platonic ordinance is suddenly revoked, and spontaneously our separated halves spring back once more to their right predestined wholes. And what is contained in these supreme transports, as hollow of thought as they are deep charged with feeling ? A single spirit of splendour, we hunt in triumph through forests of flame. We are the wind that bends the flower at the hour before day-break, the wave that shakes the firm rock, the forked lightning that cleaves the tree, down, down to the matrix of its roots. It is you that I am possessing. It is you to whom I give myself utterly, utterly. As two we met, but as one we are parted. The earth was our mattress and the grass leaves our wedding sheets. Above the sycamore the moon held her peace, while in the noonday over the woodland tree-tops the sun staggered with joy—Oh ! my love, my love. Oh ! bird that crosses the ferny glade ! Oh ! Impalla leaping

247

free in the wide plains ! I follow, I worship, careless of all but you, of you fearfully visible.

Sweet lover come, renew our lovemaking
Within the garden where the light birds sing,
Until the watcher sound the severing.
Ah God, ah God, the dawn ! it comes how soon.

Dittany would not consent to let me leave by myself, but, fetching a long blue dressing-gown from the summer-house, she accompanied me a little distance. My way lay along a path through a ripening cornfield. How white her cheeks looked in the cold air, as white as frost on snow. Surely, I said to myself, as she came up to me, she *is* the fairest lady who ever did woman's deed. We walked hand in hand. She was wearing sandals and her feet were soon soaked by the dew. She was also stung by a nettle. ' Out Nettl', in Dock, in Dock, out Sting.' As I knelt before her with the wholesome leaf I noticed that she was shivering and this made me fear she might be catching cold. ' You must go back, Dittany,' I said. ' We must say good-bye ' and there in the middle of the listening spears of corn I held her in my arms. Her cheeks were as chill as dawn fruit. As I kissed her my eye caught sight of a poppy and I presently went to pick it for her. ' Do you know,' she said shyly, ' everything red shows black in the moonlight but, in the morning, it wears its own colour again ? ' As she spoke with a movement graceful as a curtsy she let her dressing-gown of watchet blue fall open a little, so that I could see that the wild flower's colour was on her white nightgown.

' I shall never be sorry,' she said. Again I held her to me without speaking. Over and over again I kissed her, over and over again with tears in my eyes I told her how deeply I loved her, that I wished we need never part, not even for a moment, that I could live with her for ever. ' Live with you anywhere,' I said ; ' in a goose-stable ! '

She smiled, and ' where is the goose-stable ? ' she asked with a look that was tender, and half-mockingly she repeated the verse :

> *I'd rather be Childe Vyet's wife,*
> *The white fish for to sell,*
> *Before I were Lord Ingram's wife,*
> *To wear the silk so well.*

' Dittany,' I said, ' you will write to me, won't you ? Your letters will be all I shall have now.' She promised, and with a kiss on both her eyes, I said ' Good-bye,' and began running along the footpath towards the stile that stood between the long-shadowed elms. But I had gone only a few yards when I stopped and came back to her.

'Dittany,' I said, 'darling Dittany, you are not in love with anybody else, are you?'

'Don't tease me, Lulu,' she replied, and then at once we parted.

27

When mass was sung, and bells were rung,
And all men bound for bed,
Lord Ingram and Lady Maisry
In one bed they were laid.

BALLAD

S T. BARTHOLOMEW BRINGS IN THE COLD DEW. I DID
not see her again until November and then only for
a few hours one stormy afternoon. She had gone
with her mother and father to Capri. At first she
wrote to me regularly, letters in which there was always
something to reassure me of her love. She reminded me
of our day on the river. She wished ' that the sun had
never set upon that day '! She told me of the arbutus-
trees and of the blue and scarlet grottoes of the island,
and described the rocks supposed, so she said, to be the
rocks of the Sirens. She reported the island to be full of
magpies, ' so that I have to keep my fingers crossed almost
all the day.' She told me of summer storms and of how
the Mediterranean rollers would leap far up the precipitous
bastions of the sunny isle, drenching the myrtle shrubs and
vineyards with salt, sea spray. She told me how she would

escape and sit for hours reading in the terraced gardens of the peasantry. 'If we love as we do, nothing can ever come between us.' And then her letters suddenly stopped. I used to get up early and after my father's letters had been taken into the study by Ellen I would examine the others that were left on the slab in the hall. But neither morning nor evening post ever brought a letter from her. The soul is not where it lives but where it loves. I wrote to her continually, beseeching her to answer, begging and imploring her to answer. At All-Hallows I remember I sent off a mediæval love poem with which I hoped to catch her imagination. The tapers of Allhallowmas will last to Candlemas.

> *I have a young suster*
> *fer beyondyn the se ;*
> *Many be the drowryis (keepsakes)*
> *that che sente me.*

> *Che sente me the cherye,*
> *withoutyn ony ston,*
> *And so che dede the dowe (wood dove)*
> *withoutyn ony bon.*

LOVE AND DEATH

Sche sente me the brere, (briar)
withoutyn ony rynde,
Sche bad me love my lemman
withoute longgyng.

How shuld ony cherye
be withoute ston?
And how shuld ony dowe
ben withoute bon?

How should any brere
ben withoute rynde?
How should I love my lemman
without longyng?

Quan the cherye was a flour,
than hadde it non ston;
Quan the dowe was an ey, (egg)
than hadde it non bon.

Quan the brere was onbred,
than hadde it nou rynd;
Quan the mayden hayt that che lovit,
che is without longing.

I waited for a week to see if my Hallowmas carol was of any use and then in desperation sent a telegram. I had an answer the next morning. The girl who carried the telegram up from the village came by way of the front gate and I happened to see her, and so was able to intercept her by the laurustinus. My hand shook as I took the coloured envelope as light and thin and red as any heart-shaped sycamore leaf. I carried it down to the potato garden and climbed over the ivy wall in the corner where the bonfire used to be, and from there went to the very beech tree by the old house where my father had once surprised me giving her a kiss. Nervously I opened it and read. 'All well. Am writing to-day.'

When the letter came it contained no allusion to, still less apology for, her long silence. I seemed also to detect a certain formality in its tone. I spent the whole morning inventing explanations to relieve my misgivings. I could find no comfort and once more I began sending letter after letter with never an answer coming back. A post-card at last arrived with a picture of Vesuvius telling me she had looked into the crater and it 'had made her think of the elder Pliny.'

Again I wrote, and again there was an interval of silence, and then suddenly, on the morning of the first white frost of the year, I received a letter from Paris saying that she

was returning for two nights with her father ' to collect
things.' Her mother was to stay in Paris and then they
were going back to spend the winter in Capri. She asked
whether I could meet her under the great beech tree at
four o'clock on the first Thursday in December. I had a
little over a week to wait for this tryst and already I had
forgotten all my trouble about her not writing, excusing
her easily enough, now that I knew I was to see her again
so soon. When we were together I was sure it would
be the same.

My father had to go to his bank on the morning of this
letter's arrival and as was his custom he walked into
Yeovil. I remember on his return he confessed to my
mother that he had felt tired. ' I can't think how it is,
Mary !' he had said. My mother told me this with a
certain light amusement. ' I explained to him that it was
because he is getting old.' She had always given full
attention to my father listening to him with indulgence,
with a solicitous concern that was becoming to the woman
who had directed a good man's steps for so many years.
In the year 1914 I was given positive proof of how my
father had valued my mother's love for him and of how
lost he felt without her. During the weeks between her
death and my own sailing for Africa I spent much of
my time resting in the Terrace-Walk sometimes thinking
of my past with Dittany, and sometimes about the

continent I was preparing to visit. It was a superb August and the air of the terrace was odorous, week after week, with the scents of the phloxes and wasp-eaten apples and Michaelmas daisies. I did not know it, but these ominous war days were the very last I was ever to spend in that garden of memories. My couch faced the elder-hedge on the other side of which was the potato garden. How well I remembered as a child running there, heels over head, to look at a thrush's nest that was in one of the forked branches of the Blenheim apple tree, and in my innocence being brought up short by a different spectacle, the unusual but arresting spectacle of the second gardener, Pippard, hoary of head, shamelessly pissing in the windy April sunshine! This was the same old man who used to have a jar of cider always handy in the shade of a currant-bush in the autumn when he was digging potatoes. He would hide it under a heap of mares'-tails so that it should keep cool and so that my father should not see it. I remembered, too, how as a boy of eight or nine I used on summer nights to force myself to walk round this same lonely part of the garden thinking by so doing to breed in myself a stouter heart. How often had I not gone faltering round that enclosure, in the heavy darkness transforming all objects to objects of fright, and starting clean out of my skin at the audible rustle of leaf or at the movement of a harvest-mouse in the grass!

On that August afternoon my father suddenly appeared with a gardening basket, gardening gloves, and a small hand-fork, and kneeling down upon the gravel began prodding up the small grasses, chickweeds, groundsels, and veronicas that supported a needy existence amongst the many hard-trodden little stones. I preferred to be by myself when I was resting, so I pretended to be asleep. Presently I was aware of a curious noise. It reminded me of the sound I had once heard our black-and-tan terrier, Nip, make, when he came home with a gin on a hind foot. The second time I heard it I sat bolt up on my couch. Better children weep than old men. I looked at my father ; he was working quietly on his knees with his back to me. Again I heard it and this time I was sure it had come from him. ' Father ! Father ! ' I called, leaping up and running to his side, overwhelmed by a flood of love such as I had scarcely ever felt for him before. Large tears were falling upon the patch of ground where he was working. Indeed, the roughed-up gravel-mould was wet with tears that had been steadily falling from the grey eyes of this proud old man of countless inarticulate reserves whom not one of us had ever known to cry. ' What is it ? What is it ? Father ? ' My heart yearned with sympathy. His words came at last. ' There is nobody now to come and see what I do ! '

★   ★   ★

At luncheon the day after I had had Dittany's letter, my father told us that as he was leaving the bank at Yeovil he had met 'that worthy woman from The Grange.' 'What did you say to her?' my mother asked. At another time this might well have annoyed my father, as, like all shy people, he did not care to be questioned about his conversations, but he was in very good humour that morning. 'I asked the good woman about her nephew,' he said, 'and she told me he was in Paris, but was going to spend the winter in the island of Capri.'

In a flash I knew everything. I had been mad not to have guessed it before. Whenever such suspicions had entered my head I had summarily dismissed them. Surely if Randal had been in Capri she would have told me. And yet sitting there at the dining-room table helping myself from a dish of artichokes and looking at the familiar books in the bookshelf—the flower books on the top shelf, *Nada the Lily*, *Adventures at the North Pole*, *Eastern Hunters*, *The Fifteen Greatest Battles of the World*, and the Bibles on the bottom shelf, I knew for certain that this was the true explanation of her silence. It made all clear. Silence was her way of treating any embarrassing crisis. Her not writing was her way of telling me. She would never have had the heart nor the courage to say outright : 'I don't love you any more. I now love Randal.'

When once luncheon was over I began walking. I did
not rest, I walked on. I suspected Dittany's mother of
arranging it all. I have cured her from lying in the
hedges, quoth Mummy, when she had wed her daughter.
It was a good match. The mere thought of Pixley enjoying Dittany's lenience, teaching her now in the morning, now in the afternoon, to be a woman of ' good
marriage,' threw my mind into a state of turmoil. And
yet could I blame her ? If there had been vetches in
my dove-house it would have wanted for no pigeons.
What had I to offer, a young man with no money and no
profession ?

There they were together, day after day, as she and I
had never been. If he made any mistake in his wooing
he always had a second chance.

He saw her *every day*. The time that I had spent with
her I could easily reckon up in hours ; for him each poor
hour of mine would very soon be a whole day. If I
added up all the words I had ever heard her speak their
total sum would not be so many as he had already heard,
not by thousands upon thousands. I groaned as I walked
along the frozen lane by Trecease Copse between orange-
red spindle hedges. If the bed could tell all it knows it
would put many to the blush. I could not bear to think
of it, to think of it. I felt that my life was being ruth-
lessly pillaged of what was most precious to it. I could

never accept common existence with the same confidence again. My philosophy was shaken to its foundation.

Of course she had loved him from the first moment she had seen him. I had always subconsciously suspected it, and now I knew it. Yet if this were the case, would she have given me that night ? And yet she might have done this too, with intention. It would be like her. She *had* loved me, she loved me perhaps still, after the fashion of a false true-love, and she would think in her girl's heart, if I am going to leave him, going to desert him I would feel happier, if I had given him this absolute proof of the authenticity of the love I had for him. Can a mill go with the water that's past ? The rooks as they traversed the sky above my head uttered melancholy wintry caws as if they could find little grain in the frozen corn lands.

★   ★   ★

The day of our meeting came. It had been raining all the morning and at lunch time when I entered the nursery to wash my hands a wind was still gustily vexing the branches of the acacia while a bare brown spray of the clematis kept tapping fretfully, ceaselessly, against the window-pane ! I never forgot that fragmentary interval of time, with its insistent tapping. All my life what

260

had to do with that occasion, down to its minutest detail, was to be retained by a caprice of memory in a precise mirror of retrospection—my sensation of handling the large, cold, clean washing-stand vessels ; the smell of the Vinolia soap mingling with the smell of roast meat coming up from the kitchen, the sound of rain outside, and a vague sense of the peculiar desolation that belongs to garden trees when they scatter leafless twigs upon the rank, old grass of wintry lawns.

28

Where is the pride of summer,—the green prime,—
The many, many leaves all twinkling?

.   .   .   .   .

Where is the Dryad's immortality?

THOMAS HOOD

I SAW HER COMING AFTER I HAD WAITED ONLY A FEW minutes and, as often before, I went light foot to meet her. The very instant I was in her presence I was under the sway of my old passion. Neither of us spoke. I held her in my arms, looking at her, and looking at her. She was wearing a fur coat and out of it her neck rose fragile as a saffron crocus out of autumn moss. The smell of her skin and hair and of all her girlishness, came to me as though we had kissed but yesterday. It was the smell of a nursery with sweet-briar at the window, with the balmy fragrance of idle summer weather lightly troubling the airy spirit-like curtains.

When I let her go she was crying. Her cheeks were wet and she was eager to find her handkerchief, 'I only have an hour and a half,' she said. I could not be angry, so poignantly did her words remind me of our old meetings when as if to make doubly sure that not one minute would be wasted, we had always been so scrupulous to calculate the exact amount of time we were going to have together.

'We will go,' I said, 'to the old place at the very top of Hedgecock so as to be there when the rooks come in.' She took off her glove and put her hand into mine, and together, side by side in the darkening autumn afternoon we climbed up through the wood in which during the leafy months we had spent so many of our happiest hours. 'Dittany,' I said, 'why didn't you write to me, how could you leave me without any letter week after week?'

The long intervals of anxious waiting and daily disappointments that I had suffered that autumn, together with the certainty that she was hiding her relationship with Randal from me, disposed me, fool that I was, to reproach her. As I upbraided her in the November wood, her shoes kept slipping on the damp hillside. She made no defence, but presently I saw that she was once more crying, crying as though she went in woe by the way of Weeping Cross. 'He travelled to Capri, he has been with you in Capri.'—'Only towards the end.'—'He is going to go back there?'—'Only for a little time.' I was furious, tortured, mad with jealousy; and so fantastically did my brain work under its stress that

263

the famous picture gallery of Tiberius came into my
mind, a gallery, so it was said, founded and endowed
by the Emperor himself so that none dwelling in
the island of Capri 'might want a pattern for the
execution of the lewdest project that might enter his
head.'

We reached the mossy wall. I had found a scrap of
Samian pottery that a mole had cast up on to its earth-heap
at the Frying-Pan end of Ham Hill and I had had this
terra-cotta shard set in silver so that it could be worn as a
pendant, and now in a hope that I might change my own
mood and make her glad again I took the trinket from my
pocket and gave it to her as a Candlemas bond, wrapped
up in cotton wool and tissue paper just as it had come
from the Yeovil silversmith. Far-fetched and dear-bought
is good for ladies. Never did an April day change more
suddenly than did Dittany's face. She was always like
that. She responded like a child to any present. However deep her dejection, it would be gone from her in
an instant if a gift was put unexpectedly into her hand.
This love-token was one that I knew would please her
more than any that I could have devised. The locket-like
ornament was fitted with a secret spring so that its back
could be made to open, revealing the engraved words,
'God have mercy on all lovers.' I showed her the
working of the spring, and where the pendant must

264

be pressed. She took off her other glove to examine it more closely. It was this fortunate gift which prevented our last walk together from being absolutely ruined by my crabbedness. I never could be angry for long when I was with her, and even if he *had* kissed her, what traces of his love could I find on her pale face?

> *Lips where all day*
> *A lover's kiss may play,*
> *Yet carry nothing thence away.*

She read the engraved words on the hidden shield of the trinket. ' Where do those lovely words come from ? ' she asked. ' From an old song,' I said, ' which my brother John taught me once when we spent a morning reading together, in a shady corner of a cornfield somewhere beyond the Five Ashes. It is a short and simple song, I have always remembered it.' ' Say it to me,' she begged. Standing by her side I repeated the two verses, my mind transported from the fungus-smelling autumn ground to our happy summer days when each buttercup had shone yellow as a guinea and every grass-leaf in the hayfield meadows had held up light flowers to be dissolved each sunshine second into floating dust upon the breeze.

265

Pansies are sweeter, are sweeter than rue;
Cowslips are rarer, are rarer than willow;
Kiss the boy who kneels with you.
Make the cuckoo-flowers your pillow.

Death comes soon, and youth has wings;
Snatch the chance the time uncovers;
Spring alone the crocus brings;
God have mercy on all lovers!

In the dim twilight of Hedgecock she certainly did not seem to have forgotten the love that had fallen so deep between us. It was the same as it always had been. 'Forgive me, forgive me always, whatever I do,' she entreated.

The rooks had not come in yet. I soon found a suitable fir tree, easy for her to climb. She followed me up the tree without difficulty and we settled ourselves in a place where we could lie side by side on an outspreading branch, as if in a hammock. Far above our heads the ragged clouds raced across the sky. It was obviously blowing up for rain. The great west wind, the rainy wind, was sweeping in from the sea, in from the Bishop Rocks, in from the uncharted wastes of the Atlantic where masterless oceanic roarers swelled, subsided, stampeded, thundered, screamed at each other beneath a scudding sky of frenzied desolation. Before the tumult of its mighty harmonies, our tree, and all the other trees on Hedgecock, were swaying backwards and forwards with murmurings lonely and lamentable. Dittany had fallen completely under the influence of the wild oncoming night. In such an unusual cradle she appeared like an affrighted spirit out of the hollows of space, who in distress from the fury of the storm had come to a precarious harbourage upon an earth tree that, for all its ceaseless clamour, remained in the essence of its material vegetable habit, solid and sensible. She did not speak, and, looking at her oval face, I realized that she was already, as I had seen her on other occasions, carried out of herself and away from me in the brimming flood of nature's poetry. At such moments it was as if she escaped from me beyond all possible recall and was drifting, drifting with no will, across the cloud-like shifting edges of some lightless, lawless, inhuman region, outside the circuit of place and time.

Blessed indeed art thou, O wind!
Scatterer of the wild desires.

. . . . .

Thou art the boon of my spirit, the healing of my broken sores,
Thou confessor! How shall I tell?
I am prodigal with wishes that are intensified, but must be
  kept hidden.

. . . . .

Blow, blow for ever, O Blessed Messenger of Heaven !
Blessed is the cry of the wind that fore-runs the rushing gales.

It was getting darker now ; every moment it was getting darker. From where I lay I had been able to look through the foliage down to the very fox's hole that we had visited on the spring morning when the floor of Stoke Wood had been so thick-carpeted with dog's mercury. Soon even this blot of darkness became indistinguishable. Had the animal with its small wistful visage come out upon its platform I would hardly have been able to detect its form and certainly not its red prick ears tipped with black.

As I went out in a moon dead night
I set my back against the wind,
I looked for one and saw two come.
The boughs did bend, the cones did shake
To see what hole the fox did make.

Then far away we heard the rooks. The distant clamour of that dark multitude mingled with the dolorous murmurings of the congregated trees of Hedgecock. Crying and calling, tumbling and falling, host upon host of them, the black birds approached their dizzy sleeping-stations. Down in the village streets of Bishopston, Middlestreet, and the Borough, I knew that the oil-lamps were being lit in houses of goodly Ham stone, were being lit and placed upon kitchen tables at which little girls sewed, and at which little boys, with chestnut conkers in their pockets, whittled away at forked catapult sticks, thinking of the lucky shot when yellow-hammer or bunting would fall stunned from a wintry hedge.

It was the hour when the glowing seed of Mr. Drayton's forge was being banked up and covered over for the night by his black-bearded farrier; when brown loaves, and cottage loaves, and tin-loaves were being shovelled out from Tavender's oven with a flat seven-foot-long baker's peel; when window gloving girls had reached the last twilight interval of a long day's work, and when, in every street of the peaceful village, gusty doors were being opened by tired workmen, by free stone-fisted quarry-men, yellow-breeched from the dust of the hill; by damp ploughmen from Windmill; or by farm labourers returned fresh from their jesting on the thrumming threshing-floors of Batemoor Barn.

And while the wild west winds drove the clouds over the wooded hills and shook the perpendicular pinnacles on the church tower, and loosened the well-packed slates on the Montacute House roof, and hour after hour went careering through the dizzy branches of the loftiest planes and sycamores in the Park, trees long since, from twig

269

to trunk, naked of leaves, there would be content in the sheltered hamlet under the hill. In each house where chimney smoked the aged would go up to bed to ease aching bones with fitful spells of light slumber ; and the middle-aged, strong mortised in the everyday preoccupations of practical life, would sit by the fire with legs uncrossed, contriving new plans for present gains ; while, now in this cottage, now in that, the young men of the village, loose of limb and lusty, would cast off their jackets before frockless maidens.

' It must be wild on the Atlantic,' I whispered, for always the wind seemed rising. The rooks whirled about Hedgecock just as in the old days from the nursery window, I had watched them whirl about Montacute Hill, when its trees were still unfelled. It was a long time before a single bird settled. They swept backwards and forwards. They swept over our heads, cutting zigzag sections through the air and then suddenly falling with one wing outstretched ; and never for a moment were their white beaks closed. Truly it might have been a Walpurgis night for these dark creatures, for these giddy chicken of the driving racks ! Nobody could doubt that they were, each one of them, experiencing through blood, bone, and feather some strange ecstasy, every quill of them tingling to the whistling squalls of the strengthening tempest, each air-filled bone of them full of the storm's

frenzy. Dittany's remote mood had given place to one
of passionate, fully conscious heed. Each time the dark
multitudes swept down upon us she would press my hand
as though for protection. The rooks had communicated
their winged agitation to her, and truly it was extraordinary to have these thousands of land-fowl, black
as devil's pigeons, tumbling down upon us, darkening the heavens like living thunder-clouds, now sweeping along with the wind-storms, and now against
them, flapping distraught above the little Somerset
mountain, as might a funeral covering caught up
suddenly in a hurricane from the top of a dead giant's
tumulus.

At last they settled, a number of them, upon the very
tree where we were. By putting out my hand I could
have touched one hopper-crow, as, with the humped back
of a little old clergyman, it addressed itself for its night's
rest. We kept absolutely quiet. They seemed not to see
us or to suspect our presence, so accustomed were they
to each ritual sequence of their night-time habits. It was
soon so dark that I thought we might have difficulty in
climbing down. Except for the grieving of the branches
and the shrill plaints of each fretful gust as it whistled by,
I could hear nothing. Never could we have guessed that
so many bowed craniums were so close to us, heads of
birds old and young, dreaming of fertile ploughlands,

271

dreaming of swaying attic nests, and of the shrieking of the skies !

I whispered to Dittany that it was time for us to go, and she nodded. Our very first movement sent all the rooks into the air again, and we were well out of the wood before there was quiet. It now began to rain. The tormented water lashed against our foreheads. The lanes were so dark on that moonless night that we had difficulty in finding our way to the turnpike road. ' What a place to part in with so many witnesses,' she whispered.—' Did not a rook play the clerk and sing ' Amen ' in " Who killed Cock Robin " ? ' I asked her, and she did not miss my bitterness.—' Llewelyn,' she said, ' we never will part, not really.

" I will come back to you and you to me;
When the poplar-trees blow white and the rooks fly home,
And the fishermen draw their nets out of the sea;
I will come back to you and you to me." '

The words came to my ears through the drenching rain, but I could not be placated. ' It is too late for you now,' I shouted back, ' to hope to comfort me with poetry, with a verse of poetry, and then to go off with your new love with everything between us forgotten.'— ' You mustn't, you mustn't speak like that—you really must not. You'll make a quarrel with me at the very last. Listen, Lulu,' she said gravely, 'I am going to have your child.' Immediately I felt myself possessed by an extraordinary sense of exultant victory, far beyond anything that I could have imagined possible, deep, hereditary, and as if my very bones realized that the frontiers set by death had been broken down. I did not seem to mind anything now. My love for Dittany was fulfilled. There was a lasting pledge between us. Our love would not be able to fade away into a fabled memory with nothing to show where we had been together, not one real leaf from our silver woods to hold between finger and thumb. I should perhaps live to see this child of our love grow up, to see again the darling being of Dittany in its tones and gestures and in the delicate mettle of its finite body.

'I don't know when to tell my mother and father and Randal. But my anxiety can never, not for a moment, hurt my joy. You are really always with me because of this,' she said. But at that moment I shuddered, suddenly beset by the strongest premonition of disaster.

'I don't believe that the child will ever be born.' I spoke the words as though under compulsion.

'Why do you want to frighten me, now when we have come to our very last moment together?' she said.

I took her into my arms. I could feel her trembling.

273

The black rain of that foul, moon-blind night swept against us. It was so dark that we could see neither hedge, tree, nor field-gate. We clung to each other in the drenching darkness.

29

There shall neither a shoe gang on my foot,
Nor a kaim gang in my hair,
Nor e'er a coal nor candle-light
Shine in my bower nae mair.

BALLAD

SHE WROTE TO ME MUCH MORE OFTEN THAN SHE HAD done in the autumn. Randal was staying in a hotel in Anacapri, she told me. They saw each other every day. I knew he had won her.

Thus will I fold them one upon another :
Now kiss, embrace, contend, do what you will.

For days I would be tormented with jealousy, but I was fond of him, and that always made it more easy for me to think of them being together, ' knowing ' each other, as the Bible says. Birds must have meat however fair their feathers, she loved him and he loved her, and he was better able to make her happy, and she was going to have my child, so why couldn't I let her fly free, without recriminations ?

A letter came telling me that she was going to marry Randal.

' I love him deeply. He is so gentle to me. He is so much himself and no one else. It is often diffi-cult to understand him, but he is always imaginative and very, very sensitive. I have told him everything. He understands, and promises that he will always allow us to see each other and *never separate* us. He says that he will father our child, and that it will be as dear to him as if it were his own child, and that we shall live at The Grange where you will be able to see it as often as you like, and *me* too. We are going to be married at Candlemas, on my birthday. Do, do try to be fond of Randal and to forgive me. I know I am going to be happy.'

There was always something unpredictable about Randal Pixley. He had an erratic genius peculiar to his own odd character, his attitude to Dittany's pregnancy was exactly in his style—highly civilized and contemp-tuous as always of the usual codes. I have never ceased cherishing a kind of hero-worship for this man whose magnanimous conduct so constantly put me to shame.

> *The rarer action is*
> *In virtue than in vengeance.*

Whenever I am at a loss to imagine how the rivalries of love will in a freer society become more civil I have only to remember how sympathetic and understanding this remarkable youth was to Dittany and to me.

At Candlemas cold comes to us. I did not hear any more news for ten days, and already I began to feel anxiety and the old sense of impotent exasperation. I walked a great deal, and one afternoon I wandered into Stoke churchyard. It was a favourite haunt of mine. I liked to read the names of the more consequential people lying under the magnificent altar-tombs of carved Ham Hill stone, and found a pleasure in sauntering past the innumerable mounds that were sunk almost level with the churchyard sward, green grave-mounds of people about whose deaths none could now be sad, for so long had the winds been blowing over their resting-places. That afternoon I went to the churchyard rubbish heap and occupied myself in poking at it with my stick. I turned up several scraps of human bones, one great yellow legbone and several little bones, white and tiny as a lace-maker's pillow-weights ; belonging, perhaps, to a human foot.

It was not yet actually raining but it was one of those afternoons, common enough to the Montacute district in the autumn, with a warm south-west wind driving grey clouds pell-mell over Ham Hill, and over the soaked fields, dripping orchards, muddy lanes, and cow-mired barton yards of South Somerset. The old sexton, I noticed, was at work upon a grave near the eastern wall. Farewell, fieldfare ! It was the very wall below which Dittany and I had often walked in bright summer sunshine, coming out of the Stoke Wood by the deep-sunken lane, so happy together that we scarcely noticed the Herb-roberts spreading their aromatic crooked stems so luxuri-antly out of the ancient interstices of the damp churchyard wall. I knew the sexton. He was a costive character and yet could be merry too in his own cunning way and especially on the subject of man's mortality. When scything the churchyard grass in June he himself could look Death's very double, so lean was his figure, and so tight was his wrinkled skin wrapped about his skull with two gag-teeth protruding from shrunken gums, and he, in wide swishing swathes, laying low at every stroke so many fair flowers. He was standing now knee-deep in the long hole he was preparing.

' Yes,' he began, ' I've a-buried twenty score if I've a-buried one, and once I've a-buried 'em, the living don't mind 'em no more than a rush. They silent mourners may pester me for a year wi' graveyard flowers and then, same as with the rest, all be forgotten. The living don't hold be the dead no more than the dead do hold be they what can lick a dish, is what I do say, and see how the dear departed do couch thick in this here tidy Zunday-at-home of mine, arse to arse, as handy to each other a man mid say as Good Friday tatties down in allotment. No-thing will fill the eye of a man proper-like but a handful of dirt. I have a-tucked all sorts in and no mistake. Now it have been a babe no longer than a butter-pat I've a-put to bed with a shovel, and now a bridal maiden what ha' never know'd what it be to be handled by a man any sense, and now an old 'ooman catched all sudden-like over her stewpan. Oh! death he be artful—he takes 'em all fashions by head or tail, don't trouble he which end, and I reckon that they what don't look for 'un be in greatest danger. Threatened folks live longest. Look see ! I buried poor old Ben Pod a week come Thursday and he had been sitting safe-like in Fleur-de-Lis along be I the very evening afore he died. His missus, mind, had been a bed-rid for a twelve-month and more, and yet it were Benjy, hale and hearty, to whom call did come first, and how thic old bitch would torment en day and night wi' her tongue, as pricking sharp as a wopsy's stinger ! He were a-tied to a sour crab-tree and that's the truth o't. 'Twere all the same to her whether he were alive or whether he were dead, she'd gi' 'en gee-up ! They always kep an old joint-stool nigh to the old 'ooman's bedstead and Benjamin being a took short on Sunday morning says to hisself, " Woon pot be the same as t'other for thic little job," and sits hisself down. When neighbour did come in, there he still were, a-poked up stiff and stark like any coronation king on throne and the old 'ooman a-snoring by 'is side. " Moll ! Moll ! thy old man been and passed away on night commody," neighbour Bessie holla'd out, waking she up, and all the old 'ooman did were to turn on to her side and wi' half-closed eyes say all sleepy-like, " Be the old shitter dead, then ? " And that's what we all be, come to look at it. Shitters ! That's what we be, young and old. The witch 'ooman knowed the truth o't and that's flat. The youngster wi' his marbles in the road, the dairy-maid with cheeks o' red, the squire in 'is girt house a-taking o' his renties as fast as a' can close fisty, there bain't a penny-'orth of difference atween 'em all. We be all mommets o' dirt and when our ghosties be shifted we be laid in dirt and God Almighty have mercy on our souls and bring 'em to 'is blessed 'ome, thic girt mansion what wold Parson do tell of on Zundays, after he've a-been so busy a-measuring the lamp-oil, less his ole sexton might have a-stole a ha'porth for a drap of sommat to cheer 'en on through this 'ere vale of tears.'

I listened to the sexton's racy soliloquy with astonishment, thinking to myself how close to the bone of life his mind cut. The green mildew on a cross of white Italian marble near the half-dug grave seemed to set a seal upon the truth of his reflections. The mantle of emerald-coloured dampness had all but obliterated the pert economical letters R.I.P. at the bottom of its shaft. Who could keep a tally or even come to a just conception of the neglected populations under the sod ? Yet merely to remember the sunny summer hours I had spent with Dittany seemed a justification sufficient for all. To-day is ours : to-morrow God's. Life is love, the love that belongs to the natural earth. We are fools if we look for what is other. Who live so merry or make such sport as they that be of the poorer sort ? It is envy and pride that pull old England down, envy and pride and the contempt for the simple pleasures of the senses, and more than all, the senseless shameless scramble for gold. Let boys and girls make love with free hearts. He that is a wise man by day is no fool by night. Let men and women in middle life joy over and cherish the children their love has begotten ; let the old sit in the sun, on benches, on footpath stiles, on fallen timber, and under ivied walls, well sheltered from the east wind, content with a morsel of bread and with their meditations upon a past that is fading from memory. The whole span of a man's life is as brief as a blackbird's whistle on a cockle-loft roof, and death is an eternity with no crack of doom to break in upon its monotone of silence. What are we but ' mommets of dirt ' ? as the old sexton said ; and yet, and yet for one hour, who can gainsay our laughter, our subtle wit, our capacity for pleasure beyond the endow-

ment of all other animals treading on mould and grass ?
'Mommets of dirt' we may be, yet mommets with
imaginative attributes reckless and royal and a supreme
gift of sensuality.

What then is the ground of the whole matter ? Life
is to be enjoyed for its own sake as it was in the days of the
heroes, enjoyed by eating, by drinking, by tending our
vineyards with goat-skin caps on our heads. 'Common
sense wills that every wight should work in ditching or
in digging, in teaching or in prayer. Life active or life
contemplative.' And what pleasure, deep as nature herself, can be had from nurturing our children and watching
them play and grow under our eyes, and what whirling
measures of transport, lifting us clean out of our sulky
sloth, may be filched to a purpose, when in the pride of
our manhood we lie with Penelope on her bed of shining
wool, with Calypso on her banks of seaweed, salt and
dry ; or with the dread Goddess Circe in her glorious
chamber of wide island prospects ! The nobleness of life
is to do thus.

For age after age in solitary cells of dissolution hosts
upon hosts of dead men lie silent and senseless in the cold
clay. Their tongues will wag no more, there is mould
in their nostrils, and their eyes are empty of light. There
is gravel in their mouths and their ear-holes are waxed
with the fat of worms. Above them in the blessed light

of the sun a privileged few spend brief periods in the land of the living, men and women of tears and laughter empowered with a rash freedom of seventy or eighty years. Foolishly the most of them waste their days in stupefying their heads with frozen words and in shackling their limbs with fetters of gold ; the rest, a few, free in a fabled Cathay, move entranced ; there is buttercup dust on their shoe-leather and in their hearts the fond golden follies of laughing Aphrodite.

> *When we combine therewith,*
> *Life's self is nourished by its proper pith.*

My meditations were now interrupted by the sexton's voice. He had just heaved up a weighty spadeful of rain-sodden earth and with one of his skinny arms resting on his shovel's wooden handle he was obviously ready for further brabble. ' Terrible sad news about thic poor maid what used to live in these parts.'

I gave him only half my attention. ' About whom ? ' I asked.

' About thic Stoone maid,' he said. Even then I did not connect what he said with Dittany.

' She what have died out in they foreign lands, so word did come to Emmy this morning. She were a good-hearted maid by all accounts, always the same whether she spoke to rich or to poor, but she won't heel down no

283

more shoe-leather, that's certain, nor sippy no more at kitchen broth neither, the more's the pity.'

I tried to question him. He knew nothing more than that news had come of her death. The baker had told his daughter, he said.

30

A fool can dance without a fiddle.

PROVERB

TWO DAYS LATER I RECEIVED A SHORT LETTER FROM Randal. He told me that Dittany had slipped on one of the steps cut in the precipitous cliff of Anacapri. She had been walking a little in front of him, and, suddenly slipping, had slid over some twenty of the jagged stones roughly cut into shape so long ago by Phœnician traders. She had suffered some internal injury and had died the next morning. The letter ended :

> ' I shall stay here for another week perhaps, trying to do what I can for her parents and after that my plans are uncertain. At Easter I may or may not return to The Grange. There is no more to be said. She asked me to give her love to you.'

A fortnight later I heard that he had shot himself in a hotel at Naples. He left me in his will the sum of one thousand pounds and this money made it easy for me to go to British East Africa in 1914.

Many years after, in 1928, I entered one afternoon the

hillside cemetery in Capri where the two lie buried side by side. I found the graves were at the top of the sloping enclosure, almost immediately under the road that winds its way up to Anacapri. I stood by the whitewashed wall, populated with darting lizards, and surveyed the brown and ragged cliffs of the mainland coast opposite. The smoke of Vesuvius trailed across the sky.

> *The dweller in the land of death*
> *Is changed and careless too.*

Heathcliff had lifted the lid of Catherine Linton's coffin twelve years after her death and when he had looked long at her face he returned to his old nurse to say, ' *It is her yet.*' Would Dittany's face, I wondered, lying so close to me, be hers yet, after eighteen years, that face that has haunted my mind through every flying season in every continent I have visited? How sweet to my sight, how darling to me for ever had been her features, the features of this girl, trodden down by no oxen of the blacker sort, who had come and who had gone, with a measurement of life no longer than that of a woodland bird!

There they lay under the sunny Mediterranean sod, a princely pair of lovers, he, with his courtesies and proud reserves and prouder magnanimities, all come to naught. Never again would those who loved him marvel at his unaccountable spirit flashing upwards between recurring

286

intervals of easy-going sloth ; no longer would they stand confused before the dreamy aloofness and simple integrity of his nature. And she, the one sepulchred for ever by his side in the island rock, with the strangeness of her magical eyes destined to turn in the long ages to shining gravel, her wise duplicities at an end ; the gentleness of her nature, her yielding sensuality, her childish irresponsible laughing happiness when nobody knew why —to be glimpsed, and then experienced never, never again.

Through the sharp hawthorn blows the cold wind.

Oh ! Dittany ! Dittany ! how you tore at my heart —yet how I have loved you ! You were to me a fairy from the land where the fox lane leads, whether the rain was blowing cold against your cheeks, whether your hair beneath your tam-o'-shanter was ridged with springtime hail, or whether your forehead was bright with the sunshine of a celandine bank where the sloe-trees were white as clouds.

People have often wondered how I came to be so obsessed by life's instability. It was in Africa that I consolidated my philosophy, but it was Dittany and her death that prompted my dangerous scholarship. A man of gladness seldom falls into madness. I remember well, as I rode in Africa on Ramadan, meditating in my heart crafty conclusions. The wind in a man's face makes him wise.

287

Often have I heard relate
And for truth to tell,
No one has a joy parfaite
But comes of loving well.

Dittany was dead, she would never come again. I could stand calling and calling in the woodlands and withy-beds of Montacute, but never, never would an answer come back to me from her through the trembling leaves and over the rain-wet summer meadows.

Unto one end all sorrow flows.
Helen and Iseult long ago
Have gone—And go shall we.

At the most the years left to me would not be as many as the autumn apples in an orchard sack. Let me then with the utmost deliberation treasure and measure out the days that still remained, holding myself aloof from the crowd's illusions, and let me be, at need, more strictly controlled than the most starched moralist ; that is, though able to give myself utterly to every indulgence when chance offered, able, no less, to be master of myself at a moment's notice when such discipline was called for ; emulating not only the luxurious ex-travagances of Nature, but her austerity, her chastity also.

I was over thirty when these resolutions entered my head. An old ox will find a shelter for himself. I recall exactly when and where it was that the strong conviction of my unalterable faith came upon me. At the time of the light rains, like a good shepherd, I used to do all the tailing of the lambs myself, usually in the very early morning when, because of the cold, the animals would not lose so much blood. This would often mean my riding away from the homestead in the small hours of the new day. I was returning from one of these early expeditions with my ears still tingling with the outcries of the little creatures—symbols of salvation—whom I, with hot irons, had been so brutally mutilating, when, as I came through a valley with dead craters to the left and right of me, I found myself behind a herd of zebra. There must have been more than a hundred of them galloping in front of Ramadan as the sun rose, the alternate bands upon their hides gleaming with the level rays. I cantered behind the herd for several miles, their striped backsides, fat as butter, bounding up and down as they fled before me, now wildly barking, now lowering their heads and flattening their ears as they dashed through the lilishwa bushes. Life upon earth requires qualities of the most contradictory kind. It requires the stoutest heart, the slyest wits, and the nimblest heels. Those who are worthy to be told the truth should be told it ; the rest should be deceived at every chance without scruple or remorse. Firmness of spirit is necessary, and compassion always, but also a strong and stout determination to put life to the test upon all occasions without fear. Danger and delight grow out of one stock. Of two alternatives it is often wiser to select the more adventurous. Virtue and chastity that are won at the price of twisting our natures are in no way superior to degrading vice, in no way to be preferred ! Far off is that which exists and very deep—who can find it out ? Morality must be purged of its last claim to divine sanction. It must be recognized for what it is, a pragmatic system of social accommodation varying with the customs of each epoch, and of each race. There is no pity in the clouds. This is most certain. The crooked smoke that carries our prayers up to Heaven from our cottage tuns vanishes ; it is lost no great distance above the barton poplar trees. Always we must mind earth affairs, mistrusting those men and women whose God is in the skies ; simplifying our pleasures, frank and free, to the periphery of the skin that covers our backs. Many are the rascals who study to improve our morals and make our lives less honest.

There is no absolute morality ; all is relative and each separated circumstance is like no other that ever was. There is no immortality. There is no God either ! The recognition and acceptance of these denials are the beginning of all wisdom. Only so can we hope to become generous enough, humane, honourable, and happy enough to lay the firm foundations of a Utopian existence here on earth.

31

*For like as the ground is given unto the wood, and the
sea to his flood, even so they that dwell upon the earth
may understand nothing but that which is upon the
earth.*

ANCIENT WISDOM

MY HÆMORRHAGE HAD LASTED NOW NINE DAYS
and I was awake to watch the dawn break on the
thirteenth of August. This was the anniversary
of my birth at Rothesay House in Dorchester, the anniversary also of many occasions in my life that I could
remember ; not only the birthday entertainments of my
childhood, but birthdays at Montacute as a young man,
especially one when, walking with John through a field
of unharvested oats near Windmill, we observed the
amethystine colour of the tasselled grain stems against the
glory of the sun going down behind Ham Hill. Born in
August, say all. How I had always numbered my days,
grudging the spending of every half-hour, an eager
hoarder of the very seconds of my life with a wish always
and always to live to as great an age as my fathers. It
was on this day too that I had been at the side of my

brother Willie when he shot his first lion which we had tracked together through a jungle on hands and knees. It was on this day that I sailed for America at thirty-five to make my livelihood by writing.

Throughout my illness I had been superstitious about my birthday.

This day I breathed first; time is come round,
And where I did begin, there shall I end;
My life is run his compass.

If I could live through my birthday, if I were alive on August 14th, 1933, I would, I believed, be above ground for many following years.

I saw Mrs. Lucas come trudging up the downland valley with the Chydyok post, with my birthday post. 'I do hope and pray day and night for Mr. Llewelyn,' she had said to my sister. 'I do bide and think of 'en, day and night, and do hope and hope that God Almighty will save and see.' The sun was shining strongly over the downs. On such mornings in August, children are taken for excursions. On such mornings as this I had myself set out for all-day expeditions with my father, had gone to Portland, to the Quantocks ; and on such mornings I had lifted up the slats of the Venetian blinds of Penn House to see the esplanade at Weymouth, all glittering in the seaside glare, with the old linked chains drooping from white-stone-block to white-stone-block, and little girls in sun-bonnets already following behind their nurses with spades and buckets, and the pebbles of the beach rattling under the salt wet heels of boatmen's boots, and the bay, blue as the sky, stretching away to a white-sailed frigate and to St. Alban's Head. And always in those days of my childhood, of my youth, of my manhood, long periods of life seemed still to lie before me, blindly eager as I was for earth experience.

It was in the late evening as I lay half asleep that I realized that I was going to be very ill. I felt convinced that the hour that I had dreaded all my life long had come to me at last. Everywhere in the sky the stars were appearing ; moment by moment clustering more and more thickly in the remote spaces of the August night. Haphazard thoughts began to drift through my mind.

The Jews, I recalled, were accustomed to assert that there were nine hundred and three different ways for a man to die : the easiest they compared to the lifting of a hair out of a bowl of milk and the hardest to the tearing of a thread away from a closely woven cloth. I remembered, also, a visit I had paid to an old Dorset labourer on his death-bed. It was a hot dog-day, and to reach the cottage I had passed through a garden of honesty, of hollyhocks, of Canterbury bells, of larkspur, of scarlet-runners, and flowering onions, all loud with the murmur of honey-bees. As soon as I entered the low-roofed, white-washed bedroom I realized at once that the octogenarian was greatly agitated. Under his close-cropped white head his cheeks showed unnaturally flushed. A married daughter was looking after him. ' Dad be a-dying hard,' she cried, ' and he won't die any more easy till he be laid along the grain of the floor but, mercy me ! he can't abide to be shifted.'

> Death, be thou painless,
> As our Lady was sinless,
> When she bear Jesus !

I took a chair, and at a loss how to help, I read him a psalm out of his bedside Bible as I had seen my father do so many times. ' It is they folk outside that be akeeping me ghosty back,' he remarked when I had finished, his eyes nervously fixed upon the open bedroom window. ' It be they honey-bees that be doing I the mischief, for I ask 'ee, mister, how can my soul go out o' windey proper-like wi' so many of God's childer a-staring to see 'en flit over they flower-knots ? ' In the high Alps I had been told that when death comes tardily the peasants will often carry ' the one in woe ' out of the house so that he can have the heavens clear over his head. It is a belief that the sight of the swarming galaxies will tempt the spirit of a dying man to fly free from the cumber of his corporeal dwelling, up, up to the golden City of God.

How old, how very old the night sky looked ; older than the sun, older than the oldest of the gods ! In what way may the human race be said to better the flies of a green downland valley flickering above gorse-bushes when all is at peace in the misty warmth of a September afternoon ? ' So man lieth down, and rises not, till the heavens be no more, and they shall not awake, nor be raised out of their sleep.' How rapidly my own life had gone by, and yet in spite of my illness I had managed to live handy-dandy for near half a century. To-day at cheer, to-morrow on bier. *God is a dream of dreaming shadows* were the words I had chosen as the motto for my house-wall sundial. If in truth we are but shadows, then are we constituted out of a wondrous nimble matter, out of a matter which quivers and shivers as yarely as do the sun-motes of the King's highway. Shadows of glee and of dolour, we are let loose for a spell under the old, old heavens, let loose with sensible senses upon a common earth of solid substance, to glimpse, to adventure, to experience, with minds that mirror as clearly as balls of crystal.

Calm and unaffrighted the stars were shining above the downs, downs gathered together like a stationary school of enormous porpoises, each separate round hill scriptural in the simplicity of its bare outline. Surely it should be no hard thing to relinquish consciousness in the lap of so serene a firmament. For twenty years I had fought for my life, had fought for it to the very crumbling edge of the grave, but now I would let all go.

> ' Struggle no more : let it fall—'
> Cries the moss to the ivy ;
> And the ivy answers the moss—
> ' It has fallen.'

> ' Struggle no more : let it die—'
> Cries the loved to the lover ;
> And the lover answers the loved—
> ' It is dead.'

I lay absolutely motionless. It was soon impossible for me to breathe without coughing. I could feel that there had been some fresh breakage in my lungs. The nurse pulled the string that rang the bell and Alyse came to my shelter. I was sure now that I would never stand on my legs again. I choked with blood. I could smell it, I could taste it, I could see it, I could hear it. It splashed up to the top of my skull-pan until it ran out of both my nostrils. ' See what a hook God hath put into the nostrils of that barking dog ! '

But still my eager spirit would not submit. Against my will the sinews of my heart contracted themselves to save my vital flesh from death. It had been my custom, whenever my pulse-beats were being counted, to think myself back to the quiet of our garden playhouse at Montacute. I would concentrate my mind on an imagined piece of clay far beneath the roots of the Mabelulu pear trees, a lump of clay lined and stained by an incalculable geological antiquity ; a thumb-full of yellow clay that had been exact and unaltered when Montacute House was being planned by the Elizabethans, when the Frying-Pan was being delved by the Romans, and when the last great glacial escarpment was withdrawing further and further back to the arctic regions. Now, even now, I could see the face of that immutable layer of brindled, clotted, obdurate matter which always and always had silently, thoughtlessly been present beneath the flying feet of us children. Compared with such duration our lives were nothing at all. We had been fitted with bones ingenious enough, but contrived for no long stay. Miraculously modelled images of mere intellectual dust, we were ready at the first touch of fire, of wind, of hail, to fall to pieces.

Glimpses of my life passed by me in rapid succession. Once more, as a four-years-old child, I stood in the ' Littleroom,' ready to be measured for my velvet suit by Ellen

Greenham, so excited at being alive that my mother had
to be called to stop me jumping up and down and repeating over and over, ' Happy me ! Happy me ! ' Again,
with feet as light and swift as April cloud-shadows over
young corn, I ran to meet Dittany, to meet her in ' the
green corners of the earth.'

> *For I durst sweare, and save my othe,*
> *That same lady soe bright,*
> *That a man that were laid on his death bed*
> *Wo'ld open his eyes on her to have sight.*

Again I was sitting by a canal-coal fire in New York, out
of the power of the harsh world, safe, happy, and at peace
at last in Patchin Place. Once more, on the cold hillside,
I was overlooking, at the dead hour, the mountain village
of Nazareth, that village of men's fond illusions, fairer
than a sea-shell in the moonlight under the Syrian sky.
Gone, gone, all gone.

Presently I realized that Alyse must have sent the nurse
away, for we were alone together. My fever had left me.
I felt cold, and shuddered. My mind, however, remained
clear. I was dying and I knew it. Deprived of the
residue of my days I must relinquish now my private
breath. It had come to me at last, this dread moment.
It had come but I felt no fear. Above the barn I saw
the white owl floating—my corpse owl. It was not

autumn yet, I thought. It was only August. It was my
birthday. Orion and the Pleiades would not be up till
October. 'It is the objective universe,' I thought, 'the
unplatonic universe, actual, ponderable. Look well !
This is your last hour, this the butt, the glome of all your
days.' Oh, but I had loved the earth so dearly, had loved
life so dearly—and as I thought of the years that were over,
gone as a dream, with my mind so avid and my senses so
voluptuously responsive, death seemed very desolate, and,
although I said nothing, I began to cry. I had been
taught that it is not possible for the dying to cry, that
Death dries up those pathetic founts of human pity.
Alyse bent over me. Perhaps she thought I was in
pain. 'You are all right, you are all right,' she kept
repeating.

She knelt at my bedside stroking my hand. Death, I
thought, is not as terrible as I expected. When it is
upon you, your body knows there is nothing to be done.
It is like a millet-mouse in the paws of a black panther.
In such an extremity it is best to rely upon Nature with an
absolute trust. Nature is our steadfast nurse, she teaches
the witless baby to find the nipple on the mother's pap
and she will be standing punctually by our death-bed,
ready to ease the roughness of the last scoundrel hand-
lings. There was one moment when my ' mind-horror '
struggled for the mastery and my very marrow bones

ejaculated man's primal prayer, ' Save us from eternal Death ! ' as with a shiver I remembered the extent of the fall I was then making, down, down, down from animate man to inanimate matter. How often had I known this happen to others, rejoicing always that my time was *not yet, not yet.*

To the grave with the dead, and the living to the bread. Already my voice had been taken from me. I was presently aware of a strange goose-flesh feeling, wrapping about my skin, such as I never in my life had endured before, and I found that I was no longer able to move my legs. ' I must be dying,' I thought, ' feet first, like the pygmies.' I knew that I had only a moment to try to tell Alyse what I wanted to tell her. There is no man that has power over the spirit to retain the spirit ; neither hath he power in the day of death. I could feel her arms about me, but already a great darkness was closing in upon me. My chest was heaving. A deeper blackness than ever rolled in over me, submerging my being, whelming it in a flood of utter darkness, a darkness innocent of sensation, innocent of thought ; a darkness careless of all save a blind, unenvious commerce with the dust of unending ages.

THE END

NOTE

'LOVE AND DEATH' *was begun in the late summer of the year 1933 at Chydyok, in Dorset, and finished in August 1938 at Clavadel, in Switzerland.*

The names of the poets whose verses have been prominently used are listed below, together with the number of quotations taken from each of them. I would like most gratefully to acknowledge my indebtedness to those in the tally who are still living :

Homer 1, Geoffrey Chaucer 3, John Skelton 1, William Dunbar 2, Robert Wever 1, Edmund Spencer 3, Michael Drayton 1, Christopher Marlowe 2, William Shakespeare 18, John Fletcher 1, George Wither 1, William Browne 2, Robert Herrick 1, Henry King 1, Thomas Carew 1, William Davenant 1, Edmund Waller 1, John Milton 1, Richard Crashaw 1, William Blake 3, Walter Savage Landor 1, John Keats 6, Thomas Hood 1, William Barnes 1, Alfred Tennyson 3, Walt Whitman 1, Emily Brontë 1, Matthew Arnold 1, Thomas Hardy 4, Gerald Manley Hopkins 1, John Cowper Powys 9, Padraic Colum 1, Walter de la Mare's Anthology 2, Claude Colleer Abbott 18, Philippa Powys 1, E. E. Cummings 1, Edna St Vincent Millay 2, Gamel Woolsey 8, Ballads 22, Nursery Rhymes 5, Anonymous 6.

L. P.

ABOUT THE AUTHOR

A GREAT member of a great literary family, Llewelyn Powys, brother of T. F. and John Cowper Powys, was, first, last, and always, a West of England man. Yet, he led a roving existence, driven from place to place as much by his curiosity about other lands as by the demands of a delicate constitution. Born in 1884, in Dorsetshire, and educated at Sherborne and Cambridge, he was successively a stock farmer in Kenya and a journalist in New York. He visited Palestine, the West Indies, and Switzerland, recording his varied experiences with many notable books, several of which—*Ebony and Ivory, Black Laughter,* and *Apples Be Ripe,* for instance—possess imperishable qualities, as does, most certainly, *Love and Death.*

Printed in the United States
104598LV00005B/166-177/A